**So Easy Publishing
Banbury, Oxfordshire, UK**

So Easy Publishing is a trading name of ICT So Easy Ltd.
© So Easy Publishing and ICT So Easy Ltd, 2022
The moral rights of all author(s) have been asserted.
First published in 2022.

All rights reserved. No part of this publication may be reproduced, stored in a retrieval system, or transmitted, in any form or by any means, without the prior permission in writing of So Easy Publishing, or as expressly permitted by law, by licence or under terms agreed with the appropriate reprographics rights organisation. Enquiries concerning reproduction outside the scope of the above should be sent by e-mail to info@ictsoeasy.co.uk.
You must not circulate this work in any other form, and you must impose this same condition on any acquirer.

Acknowledgements
The author would like to thank his family for their support both in the writing of this book and throughout his career.

Cover image from Shutterstock. Other images are produced by the author.

Code is syntax-highlighted using tohtml.com/python in the HomeSite style.

External links and references:
Wikipedia is free to access at point of publishing. The author and/or ICT So Easy Ltd take no responsibility for the contents therewithin.

Links to third party websites are provided in good faith and for information only. So Easy Publishing disclaims any responsibility for the materials contained in any third-party website reference in this work.

Edition 1.
Any errata will be available at
https://ictsoeasy.co.uk/book7/

Adventure Games in Python

Learning Computing One Bit at a Time
Book Seven

Contents

Introduction 1
Intent of this Book 2
What You Need 2
An Introduction to Adventure Games ... 3
Coming Up with a General Concept 4
Design a Game Map 4
Design Routes Through a Game Map ... 7
Program the Game Map 9
Design a Player 14
Program the Players 15
Design some Things 18
Program some Things 19
Create some Things 19
Design some Puzzles 25
Program some Puzzles 26
Win the Game 33
Appendix 1 36
   Program the Game Map – Files 36
   Tidy Up 40
   Add Exits 45
   Program a player 48
   Program some Things 50

Introduction

Some years ago the author discovered a book which was written many many years before that on writing adventure games; this book was written around the largely defunct language BASIC and based on computers released some 40-odd years ago.

But the book was still great. Unfortunately, the publishers did not want to be involved in a new version, so this book has drawn on that only in terms of passion and inspiration.

This book will take the reader through the process of developing a (simple) text-based adventure game in the popular language Python. You do *not* need to be an expert Python programmer to use the book, concepts will be introduced and explored, but at every stage fully working code will be provided for you should you wish. Similarly, some of the concepts are quite complex. You will be using object oriented programming, something which most school-based learners aren't introduced to fully until 16-18; you don't need to fully understand this, it is merely a toolset we will use.

You do, however, need to bring something to the table: creativity, interest, engagement and fun. These games, which have their origins in *Adventure* (written in 1975) are supposed to be *fun!*

Intent of this Book

This book, and everything that goes with it, are primarily intended for fun. It is designed in such a way as to be broken down into a number of weeks so as to be easily run as a coding club in a school or similar situation. This is not the only way they it could be used and there is no hard and fast need to stick to the weeks.

The intent is not to teach people how to program; by the end the reader may well be able to program, but that is a by-product. The intent is also not to teach good programming practice; by the end the programmers may well have identified some good practice, but they may well pick up some of the bad habits, shortcuts, and non-pythonic ways of doing things that the author has developed over 30+ years of programming. The intent – and this really cannot be repeated enough – is to have fun!

We suggest you type in the code yourself, and make reference to the appendices for code listings if needed. However, links to working code at specific points during the book, plus any errata (mistakes we find in the book!) will be available at https://ictsoeasy.co.uk/book7/ should you need it.

What You Need

This book is designed to require minimal software requirements and to be as system-agnostic as possible. Therefore, the minimum requirement is to have a working copy of Python 3 installed. The exemplar software is developed and tested on version 3.8.1 on the website replit.com. This version of Python is available on Mac, Windows and Linux (and of course the site will run on almost any system).

An IDE is needed if using a system other than repl.it. The author uses a range of IDEs and recommends programmers find one that suits them. Print screens will be provided from the replit.com interface.

An Internet connection is a good idea (and of course a requirement if you are working from replit.com). As this workbook progresses, students may find themselves making minor mistakes which can have large ramifications. It is always a good idea to work through these problems, debug the code, and fix it yourself. However, in the interest of this being a fun project, it is possible at the start of each section to start with a fresh set of code as if you had completed up to the end of the previous section perfectly. This will be made available online. Note though, it is always always always recommended to modify, fiddle with, dare we say it 'hack' the code to make it your own. Particularly if you are developing your own adventure. In this situation if you revert to the author's clean code you will lose all you own modifications!

An Introduction to Adventure Games

If you grew up in the 1970s and 1980s (and therefore like the author are very very old) or happen to have seen or read "Ready Player One", you may have heard of the games "Adventure" and "Zork". These two genre-leading games have a really simple concept:

- They are text based.
- You enter instructions to move around and/or solve problems.
- When you have solved the correct problem(s) in the correct way, you win.

These games are not the latest Call of Duty, GTA, or other mega-title. And the graphics make Minecraft look like it is in 4k. Because they don't have graphics. What they do have is playability; in the same way as reading a book can be more enjoyable than watching the movie, letting your imagination run free to decide how a game should look can be more enjoyable than bowing down to the design choices of Rockstar North or Activision.

While working through this book, you will design and make one of these adventure games. In fact, it would be particularly great if you could make two. You will be taken through, step-by-step, making a very simple one, but why not design your own at the same time?

The steps we will follow – which may or may not be the right way of doing things (in fact they probably aren't!) will be as follows:

- Come up with a general concept for the game
- Design a game map
- Design routes through the game map
- Program the game map
- Design a player
- Program the player
- Designs some things to be in the game
- Code some things to be in the game
- Design some puzzles
- Code some puzzles

We will follow an informal version of agile development; rather than designing the program to death before starting anything we will design just enough, program it, try it out, and then design the next bit. While in some cases this can lead to disastrous outcomes with programs that don't work properly, we are in the business of having fun and this gets you playing quickly! Do note, though, that this will not be a linear thing. We may need to go back and redesign things as we go through so as to keep things moving forward.

Coming Up with a General Concept

Adventure – whose full name is Colossal Cave Adventure – is based in a cave system filled with wealth. You can read more about it at https://en.wikipedia.org/wiki/Adventure_game. Zork is set in dungeons in a great underground adventure, with the objective of getting through the dungeons alive, with all the treasures, and having solved the puzzles. Again, you can read more about it at https://en.wikipedia.org/wiki/Zork.

The point is, the concept of the game is up to you. You can be as specific or as vague, as realistic or as fantastical as you like.

What about this example we're going to supply you with? Good point! Like all sensible grown-ups, the author likes pirates! So here's the back-story:

> *Ahoy me hearties! Avast! You were sailin' along yonder sea when a foul plague took upon yer ship-mates and one by one they fell into the sleepin' sickness. Ye can't sail the ship alone so ye need to drop the anchor before ye run ashore on the reef. Ye need to get to the foredeck to drop the anchor, but the ship, she is in a mess!*

You don't need a back story. I could have just said 'You're on a pirate ship and you need to get to the room where the anchor is to drop it.' But where's the fun in that? Also note that you quite often don't get told *how* to win the game – that in itself is part of the puzzle. But we need to know – otherwise we won't know how to program the solution…

Design a Game Map

The fact is that the map is the single most important part of your game. Traditionally text adventure games were split into areas you could walk between using direction commands. In the early basic games such as Haunted House these were often organised in a square grid to make the programming easier and more efficient. We can skip some of these rules if we want to although in the spirit of things, we will keep fairly close to the originals.

You will want paper and a pencil for this. Preferably a big bit of paper. A3 is ideal. Of course, you *could* design your map on computer – ours is drawn in PowerPoint for example – but to be honest this can get in the way of creativity, and we drew ours on paper first then copied them to computer just to look a little nicer for you!

So, the exemplar;

- Firstly, we had to come up with a decision on the general layout. I've decided I'm on a pirate ship, so I made the decision to have two decks.

- So we drew a ship with two decks. You can make these as fancy or as basic as you like – the design will never be seen in the game but you might give a map to your users. At this stage, simple is good!

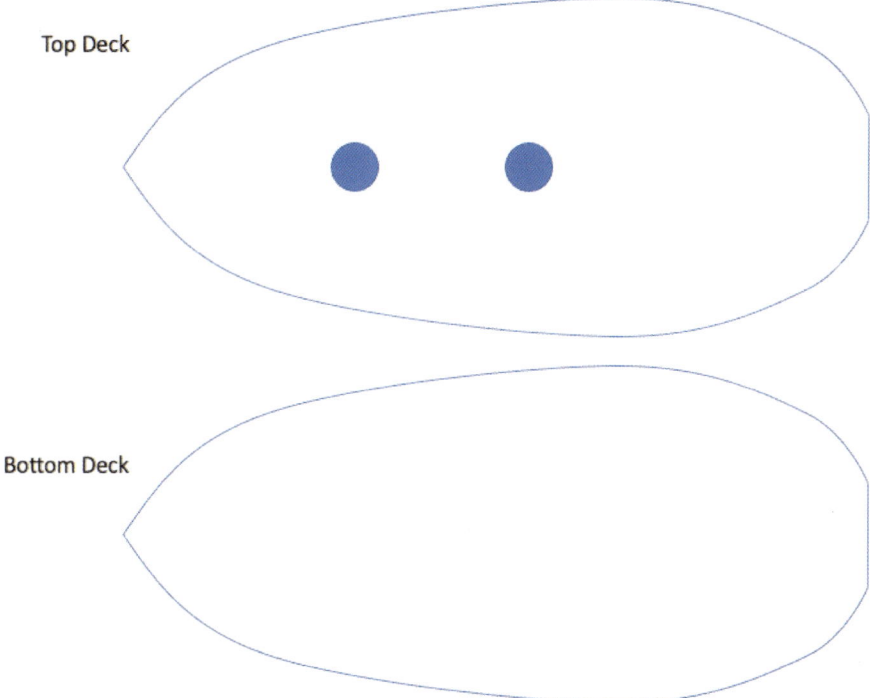

So we have two areas, top deck and bottom deck. The two masts have been marked in as well to give some context. Of course, in a real pirate ship they would go right through – but hey-ho, poetic licence!

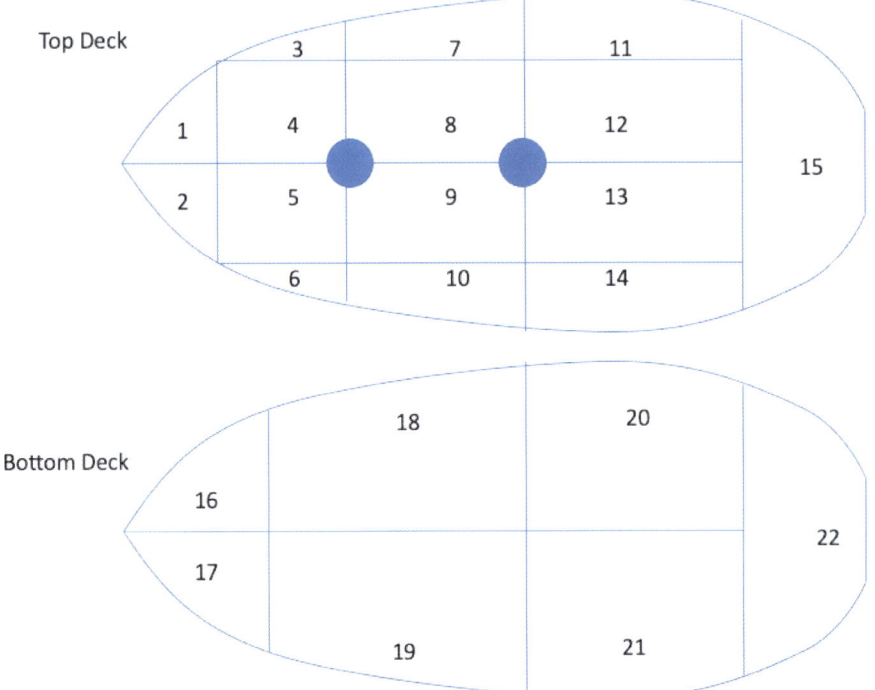

The design was then split into rooms, with each room having a name. Rather than writing the name on the picture (it will get messy fast) it is a good idea to number them on the picture for clarity and then write a list- this will form the room ID number later on:

1. Starboard Bows
2. Port Bows
3. Starboard Forebeam
4. Starboard Foredeck
5. Port Foredeck
6. Port Forebeam
7. Starboard Beam
8. Starboard Midships
9. Port Midships
10. Port Beam
11. Starboard Quarter
12. Starboard Aft Deck
13. Port Aft Deck
14. Port Quarter

15. Poop Deck
16. Starboard Forecastle
17. Port Forecastle
18. Starboard Fore Hold
19. Port Fore Hold
20. Starboard Aft Hold
21. Port Aft Hold
22. Captain's Cabin

No doubt a shippy-person will be along soon to tell us we got this all wrong - but it doesn't really matter! You might think 22 rooms isn't a lot for a game. Maybe you're right, but you're going to have to think of and write descriptions for all of these, so feel free to go wild but remember – you have been warned!

Feel free to change things as you go along. Ours has changed about five times just in writing!

Design Routes Through a Game Map

We plotted a route I wanted the player to have to take to get to the end point. This is because we want our game to end by the player getting from the Poop Deck to the anchor (in the Starboard Bows) and dropping it into the sea. If my intent was to have them collect every object or gain a set number of points, I would have to adjust this step to ensure they can get everywhere needed. This is not to say they won't have to visit other routes on the way – we just wanted to make sure that they would be able to get where they needed.

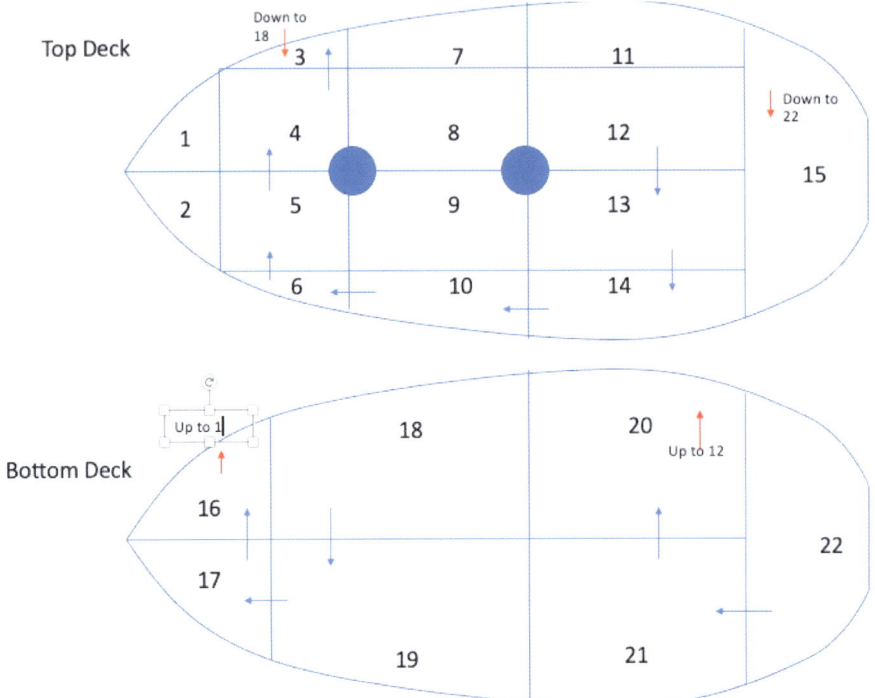

Blue arrows indicate pathways on the same level, while red arrows (and labels) indicate areas where the player will need to move between decks.

We added extra pathways between rooms. These are paths which may lead to dead ends, lead the player in circles, or whatever. It's what makes the game explorable rather than just following a set map. We used single headed arrows for one-way routes and double-headed arrows where the player can move in both directions. We also added double heads on to the routes I planned earlier. At this point you may even start thinking about some puzzles the player may need to solve and add notes on to the map while you're at it. We've added a trap that will cause the player to fall into the sea and added a secret room to make this happen. You don't need to be exhaustive – it's an iterative process!

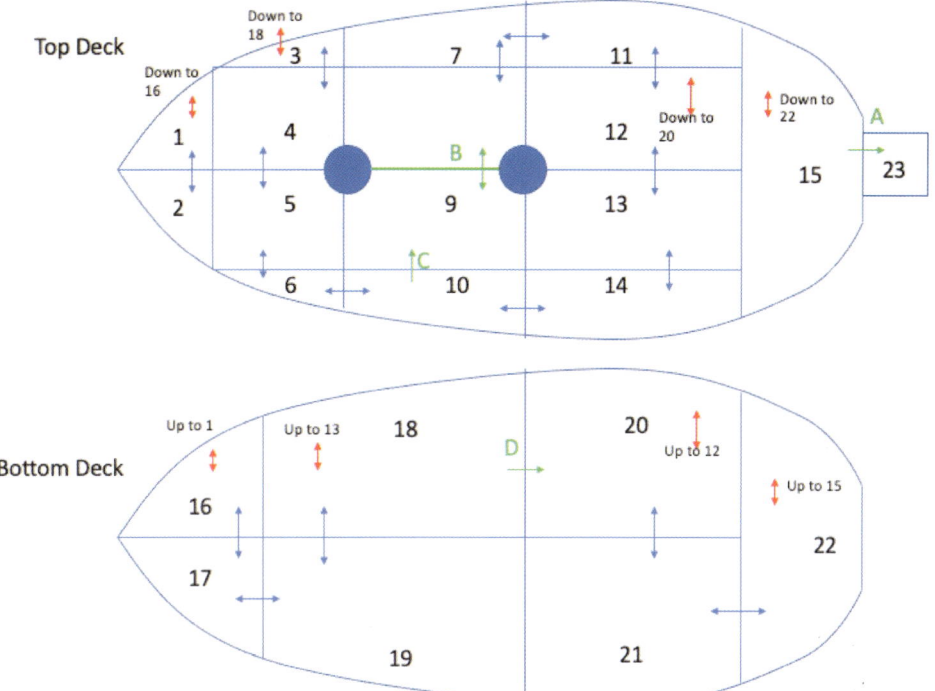

A. Is a one-way climb down to the rudder (room 23). If the player climbs down, they then slip, fall in the sea, and the game is over.
B. Is a wall which can be knocked over (probably by something we find). This will enable the player to enter a series of rooms which ends up back at room 11.
C. is a one-way exit to room 9, which means they have to solve the problem of the wall in B.
D. is a one-way exit that just means the player has to go around in circles.

If you are just following the examples, have a good look at the maps and make sure you understand it. If you are creating your own adventure game as well, go ahead and design your own map.

Program the Game Map

It's time to start programming now. Yes, it's early days in the game design world, but we need to have some fun.

What's first? Well, a little bit of housekeeping. If you are working on Python on your computer, you need a folder to keep your code in. So, go ahead and create your folder. Alternatively, if you are working in replit.com, you will want to create a folder there. We're going to call ours "Drop the Hook" since it's all about pirates and dropping the anchor (*hook* is sailor-slang for anchor).

All of our files are going to be kept inside this folder. If you're using your local installation of Python, you might want to create sub-folders for each version. If you're using replit.com, then a separate repl will be created for each one. If you are also creating your own adventure game, don't forget to create a folder for that as well.

An empty replit.com folder ready for us to work in.

We are going to use a type of programming (a paradigm) called object-oriented programming. In this type of programming, we design 'things' and we call these designs classes. Each class will have its own file. A class is a collection of code which defines what one of these things will know about itself (it's properties) and what one of these things can do (it's methods). Remember though, these classes are just designs. Later on we will *instantiate* these classes into *objects* – we bring them to life! (sort of!). By the way, you're going to get confused about objects in programming terms and objects in terms of 'things in the game'. Sorry! Just try and stick with us, it's all about having fun after all!

So; we are designing rooms. Let's think about rooms. What do we know about rooms?

- Every room has an ID number we have given it
- Every room has a name – a short description
- Every room is going to want a longer description if we look around it
- Every room is going to have some exits – so we need a list of exits
- Every room might have some things in it – so we need a list of what it contains.

What do we need rooms to be able to do? Do note that we may need to change these a bit as we go through the development cycle so it doesn't matter if we're not perfect first time. Don't tell your teacher we said this though – teachers hate agile development!

- Get and set the short description
- Get and set the long description

- Get a list of exits
- Check if an exit exists
- Add an exit (we may break a wall down to make a new one)
- Remove an exit (something could fall over blocking an exit)
- Get a list of what is in the room
- Check if something is in the room
- Remove something from the room
- Put something in to the room

Some of these things will happen when we first create the room object:

- Set an ID (this will happen only once so I have only included it here)
- Set the short description
- Set a list of exits (even if it's empty)
- Set a list of what is in the room (even if it's empty)

Based on this description, we have created a template file for the room. You can access this from our website (and a text version is in the appendices). We've called it ROOM.py. We will fill this in with code as we go along.

There are comments about what is happening in the code – don't worry if you don't fully understand it all, remember this is about fun not about understanding everything! Most of the methods have 'pass' written underneath them. This is because it is a template so we don't want to actually write all this code yet, but we want it to be there as a kind of placeholder. If you leave it empty, Python gets cross. So, we write **pass** as a kind of 'carry on, nothing to see here, as you were…'

Now what we need to do is have a 'game' - which will be another class - to hold all of these rooms. In fact, the game will have other things as well such as a status (games can be in play or not in play), and the rooms in a list, and it will also have to hold any items that we haven't yet put into rooms.

We will need to be able to add an item to the items list, move the item to a room or from a room to the 'holding' area. We will need to be able to add a room.

We will need to be able to check if we are in play, or not, and change the play status. We have again created a template file, mainly with pass in the methods, called GAME.py for you to have a look at.

Now that we have created some classes, we can go about creating a main program. We will:

- give the program access to the game and room classes (well, the templates for now)
- create a game object
- as we have programmed some of the game code, we will test our game object status methods.
- we will create a room and look at the short description
- we will change the short description and then look at it again

Of course, the main program files (which we call main.py) are accessible from our website. It is, however, better to work through this as we go.

Giving the program access to the classes means using **import** commands:

```python
from GAME import Game
from ROOM import Room
```

Creating an instance is also simple:

```python
game = Game()
```

So we have called our Game object game - note the use of capitalisation to differentiate?

To test the game status, I've told game to show us it's status, then called **flipPlayStatus** and told it to print it out again.

```python
print('Is the game running?')
print(game.getPlayStatus())
print('Flip it around!')
game.flipPlayStatus()
print('Is the game running now?')
print(game.getPlayStatus())
```

To create a Room, we create a new room object (note the capitalisation again?) with default information, and then ask it to output its short description.

```python
#Create a room (we used room 1 for an example, and it currently does not
# contain anything)
room = Room(1,'Startboard Bows',None,None)
#Look at the room's short description
print(room.getShortDesc())
```

And then we can tell the room to change its short description and output it again:

```
#Whoops - we made a typo! Change the short description and look again
room.setShortDesc('Starboard Bows')
print(room.getShortDesc())
```

All of this can be accessed from our website as "main version 1" under this section. You will have to make sure the files are saved in the same sub-folder so that main.py can access GAME.py and ROOM.py

What we need to be able to do now is add rooms to the game itself. To be able to test this there is a 'helper' method in GAME.py which prints out all of the rooms we have added. The player won't be able to use this, but it helps us!

We have created a copy of the main program, version 2, and removed the bits we just included for testing. We have now added the rooms to game and then asked game to print out the rooms:

```
room = Room(1,'Starboard Bows',None,None)
game.addRoom(room)
```

Although we can also combine this to a single line:

```
game.addRoom(Room(2,'Port Bows',None,None))
```

And you can just call:

```
game.listRooms()
```

to see what rooms the game includes so far.

Activity for you! Go ahead and add all of the rooms into the game. If you run out of time you can use our version (also in the website and appendic) but typing it yourself is always a better idea.

We need to add a bit of flavour to the rooms by adding some descriptions, adding exits, and adding some way of testing how the different rooms look.

Firstly, the GAME needs access to be able to add a long description to a room. GAME will need the room number, and the description to add, and will call the setLongDesc function of the relevant room. We can add this to GAME.py:

```
#This will add a long description to a given room
```

```python
def addRoomLongDescription(self,room,desc):
    self.rooms[room].setLongDesc(desc)
```

and while we are at it, we can edit ROOM.py to allow us to access the long description later on:

```python
#This will look at itself and give us back the long description
def getLongDesc(self):
    return self.longDesc #Just give back whatever the current long desc is
```

We can now call game.addRoomLongDescription() with the room number and the descriptions as parameters. Go ahead and put these descriptions in to your main file. Be creative, this is a lot of what makes these games fun.

Things have started getting a bit messy, however, so we can move all of this adding of rooms and long descriptions into a function called Create and store *that* in a CREATE file; then we can just call Create from the main file – much slicker!

Soon we want to be able to move around, so we also need to add all of our exits on to the rooms. We can do this in the addRoom method in Create by replacing the first *none* in each initialisation with a dictionary of directions and the rooms they go in. A dictionary is a key-value pair, so we can "look up" if "NORTH" is in the dictionary, and if it is, it will tell us the number of the room it goes to. Note we use all capitals for the directions. This is just "normal" practice for these games – but it does make our life easier later on!

Example of adding room 1 before adding exits:
```python
game.addRoom(Room(1,'Starboard Bows',None,None))
```

Example of adding room 1 after adding exits:
```python
game.addRoom(Room(1,'Starboard Bows',{"DOWN":16,"SOUTH":2},None))
```

Pretty simple, eh? Go ahead and add the other exits according to your map.

Design a Player

Of course, our game is no good without a player, is it? I mean – we need an 'us'! And just like everything else, we need to design the player. It will be an object, so let's think about what the player needs to be able to do, and what it needs to know about itself.

The player must know:
- Whether they are alive – which we can set as a **Boolean** and initialise to True

- What room they are in
- What items they are carrying – which we can store in a dictionary
- It will also need a link to the game object

The player will need a number of methods – some of which will just get or set internal variables and some which will be things it can do:
- setGame – to set the game link
- isAlive – to see if the player is alive
- kill – to make the player not-alive (for when they fall off the ship)
- resuscitate – because it's not nice to make the player permanently dead
- setRoom – to change the room the player is in
- getRoom – to check what room the player is in
- look – to look around, read the room descriptors and see what exits there are
- getItem – to pick up an item
- dropItem – to drop an item you've picked up
- useItem – to use an item that you've picked up (as long as you haven't dropped it, of course!)
- move – to move around
- getCommand – to get the command a user types in
- doCommand – to do the command that we've just got
- help – to output help on the commands

Program the Players

Phew – that's quite a lot! The initialisation code looks pretty much like the other __init__ methods we've used:

```python
def __init__(self):
    self.alive = True
    self.room = None
    self.items = {}
    self.game = None
```

We've not got items yet, so we will just ignore those for now and set them to **pass** – we so have them as placeholders ready for use later.

```python
def getItem(self,item):
    pass

def dropItem(self,item):
    pass
```

```python
def useItem(self, item):
    pass
```

setGame is pretty easy; we pass it the game object and just set the internal variable to what we pass it:

```python
def setGame(self, game):
    self.game = game
```

isAlive, kill and resuscitate are pretty easy, we just return or change the self.alive variable:

```python
def isAlive(self):
    return self.alive

def kill(self):
    self.alive = False

def resuscitate(self):
    self.alive = True
```

Similarly, getting and setting the room is just using the room variable:

```python
def setRoom(self, room):
    self.room = room

def getRoom(self):
    return self.room
```

Now things are starting to get a little tough. But that's ok because we're making progress!

Before we go too far, we need to think about what a command looks like. We're not making AI here so we can't just accept anything. To simplify things, we'll accept a single word command (a verb such as LOOK), or a two-word command (a verb followed by a noun, such as MOVE WEST). Note we can also convert anything the player enters into uppercase to make things easier to deal with.

We can write the getCommand method to get the input, convert it to uppercase, check it meets this format and then either pass the verb and option noun on to doCommand, or we can tell the user that they've been a bit of a plonker and typed in the wrong thing.

```python
def getCommand(self):
    command = input('What do you want to do? ').upper()
    commands = command.split(' ')
```

```python
    while True:
        if len(commands) == 1:
            verb = commands[0]
            self.doCommand(verb,None)
            break
        elif len(commands) == 2:
            verb = commands[0]
            noun = commands[1]
            self.doCommand(verb,noun)
            break
        else:
            print('Please enter a verb followed by an optional noun.')
            print('Enter HELP for help.')
```

doCommand is then a fairly simple if..elif..elif..else to call the correct method for each verb, and if relevant pass them the noun needed.

```python
def doCommand(self,verb,noun):
    if verb == 'HELP':
        self.help()
    elif verb == 'LOOK':
        self.look()
    elif verb == 'MOVE':
        self.move(noun)
    else:
        print('Unknown verb or noun...')
```

help is just a sequence of print statements. We need to remember to edit this when we add new commands of course!

```python
def help(self):
    print('Commands:')
    print('LOOK: Look around the current room.')
    print('MOVE <direction>: Move in the given direction')
```

look doesn't need a noun, we don't tell the player where to look, just to look. We get the room where the user is, and then get the description for this and output it. We also get the exits for which we need to update getExits() from ROOM.py to give us the list of exits. As this is a dictionary, we need to get the keys from the dictionary, and then we can format it to output nicely.

```python
def look(self):
    room = self.game.getRoom(self.getRoom())
    print(room.getLongDesc())
    exits = room.getExits()
    keys = ', '.join(exits.keys())
    print('Exits: '+keys)
```

```python
#Updated getExits from ROOM.py
def getExits(self):
    return self.exits
```

move then takes a similar start to look, but as it has the noun (the direction), we can then check whether this exists in the dictionary of exits. If it does, we can change the player's location and then look around. If it doesn't, we can output an error message.

```python
def move(self,direction):
    room = self.game.getRoom(self.getRoom())
    exits = room.getExits()
    if direction in exits.keys():
        print('\nYou move.\n')
        self.room = exits[direction]
        self.look()
    else:
        print('I cannot move that way')
```

All that is left to do is to include the PLAYER.py file from main.py, and then instantiate the player with it's initialisation information, including starting it in room 15 (the poop deck).

```python
#Create (instantiate) a Player called player
player = Player()
player.setRoom(15)
player.setGame(game)
game.addPlayer(player)
```

Design some Things

Things are things you can use. Or not use – depending on what they are. But they're *things* and therefore need to be… an object.

Our things don't really need to do much. We may choose to expand this as we go along, but for now all they need is a short description (so we can say "A hammer is here.") and a long description ("The hammer is all hammer with a handle and a hard bit you probably don't want to hit your thumb with.").

We want to be able to get and set these descriptions. We may also want some items that are there to add interest to the game, but don't actually do anything, so can't be "got". We can set a "gettable" variable which defaults to true, but can be toggled off if needed. Of course, each item will need an id as well.

Program some Things

The initialisation of our Thing class is just setting all of the variables to whatever is passed in, and defaulting gettable to True.

```python
class Thing:
    def __init__(self, id, shortDesc, longDesc, gettable = True):
        self.id = id
        self.shortDesc = shortDesc
        self.longDesc = longDesc
        self.gettable = gettable
```

By setting the gettable to default to True like this, we can just leave it out unless we want to specifically set it to False.

We need to wite get and set functions for the descriptions:

```python
#This will look at itself and give us back the short description
def getShortDesc(self):
    return self.shortDesc #just give back whatever the current short description is

#This will take the new description we give it and set this as the object's short description
def setShortDesc(self,desc):
    self.shortDesc = desc
```

The long description is of course done in the same way.

We could have had a set method for gettable, but chose instead to use a toggle; this just turns it True if it is False, and False if it is True. A very useful trick!

```python
#This will toggle the gettability of the thing
def toggleGettable(self):
    self.gettable = not self.gettable
```

There is also a getID() and isGettable() method in the full code (shown in the appendix) but you can probably figure them out from the code you've already written by now!

Create some Things

Now that we have the ability to do have some things, we need to make some things and put them somewhere. We will start off with all things in rooms, so we need to update ROOM.py to enable us to put an item in it.

When we first create a room, we set it's self.contains to be whatever is passed in to the constructor (the __init__); however, in CREATE.py we set these to None – we need to go back and change these to be a blank list, so for example in CREATE.py the line:

```
game.addRoom(Room(1,'Starboard Bows',{"DOWN":16,"SOUTH":2},None))
```

Becomes:
```
game.addRoom(Room(1,'Starboard Bows',{"DOWN":16,"SOUTH":2},[]))
```

And we need to do that for every room! Silly us!

We created a method for adding a room in ROOM.py previously, so we just need to update putIn(). A room contains a list, so we can just *append* an item to the list *contains*:

```python
#This lets us put an item in to the room
def putIn(self,item):
    self.contains.append(item)
```

We also need to bet able to get a list of everything it contains:

```python
#This will give us a list of things the room contains
def getContains(self):
    return self.contains
```

What else do we need? Well, we need to be able to check if a room contains a given item:

```python
#This will let us test if a particular item is in the room
def ifContains(self,lookingFor):
    items = self.getContains()
    for item in items:
        if item.getShortDesc().upper() == lookingFor:
            return item
    return None
```

That will just loop through everything the room contains and return the item if the thing it is looking for is found, otherwise it returns None. This means that, if something is found we have direct access to it. Note we have to convert the descriptions to uppercase since all of our nouns are upper case.

And of course, we need to update GAME.py to allow us to actually *tell* a room we want to put an item in it. You will see that the modification to addItem() is very similar to addRoomLongDescription().

```python
#This will add an object to the items dictionary
def addItem(self,room,item):
```

```
    self.rooms[room].putIn(item)
```

Let's go back to CREATE.py and create some items shall we? I've just added a hammer at the bottom for now:

```
#Add some items
hammer = Thing(1,'a hammer',"It's got a wooden handle and a heavy bit on the end. It's heavy enough to smash a wall down, or break your toe if you're not careful!")
game.addItem(15,hammer)
```

(Note the use of "double quotes" so that we can use apostrophes in the text?)

This is great, but when we run the game we can't *see* the items, so we need to edit look() to show all the items in this room. We want to see the short description and form it into a sentence.

```
def look(self):
    room = self.game.getRoom(self.getRoom())
    print(room.getLongDesc())
    for thing in room.getContains():
        print('A',thing.getShortDesc(),'is here.')
    exits = room.getExits()
    keys = ', '.join(exits.keys())
    print('Exits: '+keys)
```

This is starting to look pretty cool!

```
Adding rooms
Adding long descriptions
running the game
tick
What do you want to do? look
The poop deck (hahaha!) is the rearmost part of the ship, where
the steering wheel is located. Posh people only up there!
A hammer is here.
Exits: DOWN, EAST
tick
What do you want to do?
```

We need to be able to look at the hammer in a bit more detail. We can modify doCommand to add a lookItem() method if a noun is specified:

```
def doCommand(self,verb,noun):
```

```python
    if verb == 'HELP':
        self.help()
    elif verb == 'LOOK':
        if noun == None:
            self.look()
        else:
            self.lookItem(noun)
    elif verb == 'MOVE':
        self.move(noun)
    else:
        print('Unknown verb or noun...')
```

Then we can add lookItem(), which is going to be quite similar to look() really…

```python
def lookItem(self,noun):
    room = self.game.getRoom(self.getRoom())
    thing = room.ifContains(noun)
    if thing != None:
        print(thing.getLongDesc())
    else:
        print('I cannot find one of them!')
```

Ok, making some serious progress!

```
Adding rooms
Adding long descriptions
running the game
tick
What do you want to do? look hammer
It's got a wooden handle and a heavy bit on the end. It's heavy enough
to smash a wall down, or break your toe if you're not careful!
tick
What do you want to do? look llama
I cannot find one of them!
tick
>
```

There are a few other things we need to be able to do with our *things*, we need to be able to **get** them (pick them up), **drop** them, and **use** them. Let's add those commands to *doCommand()* for now.

```python
def doCommand(self,verb,noun):
    if verb == 'HELP':
        self.help()
```

```python
        elif verb == 'LOOK':
            if noun == None:
                self.look()
            else:
                self.lookItem(noun)
        elif verb == 'MOVE':
            self.move(noun)
        elif verb == 'GET':
            self.getItem(noun)
        elif verb == 'DROP':
            self.dropItem(noun)
        elif verb == 'USE':
            self.useItem(noun)
        else:
            print('Unknown verb or noun...')
```

And let's go ahead and build those commands, keeping in mind we will then need to go and implement some more functionality in ROOM.py afterwards.

Getting an item is a case of checking an item is available in a room (which we did in lookItem), adding it to the player's list (which we need to fix – we originally set it as a dictionary, now it's a list!), then removing it from the room's list. Dropping an item is pretty much the same but backwards. Use... well we'll just put a place holder in there for now and worry about that bit later!

Updated initialisation:

```python
def __init__(self):
    self.alive = True
    self.room = None
    self.items = [] #Changed to [] instead of {}
    self.game = None
```

A getItem() method to swap where the item is located:
```python
def getItem(self,noun):
    room = self.game.getRoom(self.getRoom())
    thing = room.ifContains(noun)
    if thing != None:
        self.items.append(thing)
        room.remove(thing)
        print('You manage to get a',noun.lower())
        if not thing.isGettable():
            print('Uh-oh... you struggle to hold a',noun.lower())
            self.dropItem(noun)
    else:
        print('You cannot find a',noun.lower())
```

Note we used drop item to make things that aren't gettable a bit more fun?

```python
def dropItem(self,noun):
    room = self.game.getRoom(self.getRoom())
    thing = self.hasItem(noun)
    if thing != None:
        room.putIn(thing)
        self.items.remove(thing)
        print('You drop a',noun.lower())
    else:
        print('You do not have a',noun.lower(),'to drop!')
```

Drop item uses the same ideas, but needed a helper method:

```python
#This will let us test if a particular item is held
#It is very similar to the room code!
def hasItem(self,lookingFor):
    items = self.items
    for item in items:
        if item.getShortDesc().upper() == lookingFor:
            return item
    return None
```

And useItem() is just a place holder – we will deal with this when making puzzles.

```python
def useItem(self,item):
    print('You do not know how to use items. Yet!')
```

ROOM.py needed one method programming:

```python
#This lets us remove an item from the room
def remove(self,item):
    self.contains.remove(item)
```

And finally, we need an immovable object to test! Sorry about the a/an problem – maybe you can think of a way to solve this?

```python
anvil = Thing(2,'anvil',"A huge piece of iron the sailors use when mending chain. Probably too big to move - it's a miracle the ship is still afloat really!",False)
game.addItem(15,anvil)
```

```
Adding rooms
Adding long descriptions
running the game
tick
What do you want to do? look
The poop deck (hahaha!) is the rearmost part of the ship, where the ste
ering wheel is located. Posh people only up there!
A hammer is here.
A anvil is here.
Exits: DOWN, EAST
tick
What do you want to do? get hammer
You manage to get a hammer
tick
What do you want to do? look
The poop deck (hahaha!) is the rearmost part of the ship, where the ste
ering wheel is located. Posh people only up there!
A anvil is here.
Exits: DOWN, EAST
tick
What do you want to do? get anvil
You manage to get a anvil
Uh-oh... you struggle to hold a anvil
You drop a anvil
tick
What do you want to do? look
The poop deck (hahaha!) is the rearmost part of the ship, where the ste
ering wheel is located. Posh people only up there!
A anvil is here.
Exits: DOWN, EAST
tick
What do you want to do?
```

Design some Puzzles

Our game is pretty playable now, we can add a bunch of items, get them, drop them, we can move around and we can look at things.

Now we need to think about our puzzles: We have two that need programming, the drop down to the rudder (and sudden, soggy death), and the bashable wall. The rudder doesn't need any *things* to solve the puzzle, we check what room the player moves into each time and if it's the rudder we make them dead. I suppose.... We could give them the chance to try again by putting them in a random room...

We can use the hammer to bash the wall, so for the that we just implement use, and if they're using the hammer *and* in the correct location, then they can knock the wall down (we just output a message and add an exit really).

It might be nice to think of some distractors. Maybe we can have a belaying-pin that does nothing, some sacks that can be split open, and a knife that does the splitting.

Program some Puzzles

To write the rudder puzzle, you might first like to try moving to the rudder. Uh-oh, the game crashes!

```
This is the rudder, the bit that turns the ship left and right.
 Mainly left - probably because of the amount of rum consumed.
It's... quite slippy...
Traceback (most recent call last):
  File "main.py", line 21, in <module>
    game.tick()
  File "/home/runner/Program-Some-Puzzles/GAME.py", line 56, in tick
    self.player.getCommand()
  File "/home/runner/Program-Some-Puzzles/PLAYER.py", line 128, in getCommand
    self.doCommand(verb,noun)
  File "/home/runner/Program-Some-Puzzles/PLAYER.py", line 102, in doCommand
    self.move(noun)
  File "/home/runner/Program-Some-Puzzles/PLAYER.py", line 88, in move
    self.look()
  File "/home/runner/Program-Some-Puzzles/PLAYER.py", line 36, in look
    keys = ', '.join(exits.keys())
AttributeError: 'NoneType' object has no attribute 'keys'
> 
```

We always start at the end and work backwards. There's something which is of type None which does not have a 'keys' attribute. This means we're trying to access the .keys() of something. If we look further up – it says line 36 of PLAYER.py and surely enough, that line is trying to join the keys() of exits. But of course the rudder has no exits – so we cannot join them!

We can use something called exception handling here – we will *try* and join the keys, if it gives us an error (an exception) we will just output a message saying there are no exits.

```python
def look(self):
    room = self.game.getRoom(self.getRoom())
    print(room.getLongDesc())
    for thing in room.getContains():
        print('A',thing.getShortDesc(),'is here.')
    try:
        exits = room.getExits()
        keys = ', '.join(exits.keys())
    except:
        keys = "None!"
    print('Exits: '+keys)
```

```
Adding rooms
Adding long descriptions
running the game
tick
What do you want to do? look
The poop deck (hahaha!) is the rearmost part of the ship, where the steering
 wheel is located. Posh people only up there!
A hammer is here.
A anvil is here.
Exits: DOWN, EAST
tick
What do you want to do? move east

You move.

This is the rudder, the bit that turns the ship left and right. Mainly left
- probably because of the amount of rum consumed. It's... quite slippy...
Exits: None!
tick
What do you want to do? 
```

That's better!

Now, we will want some random numbers, and to be able to use a delay, so let's import some modules at the top of PLAYER.py:

```python
import time
import random
```

Now let's modify move() to check if we're in room 23 and if so, output a (delayed) message and then kill the player. You can have some real fun here!

```python
def move(self,direction):
    room = self.game.getRoom(self.getRoom())
    exits = room.getExits()
    if direction in exits.keys():
        print('\nYou move.\n')
        self.room = exits[direction]
        self.look()
    else:
        print('I cannot move that way')
    if self.room == 23:
        time.sleep(2)
        print('In fact... it is *really* slippy here!')
        time.sleep(2)
        print('A bit ... tooo.... slipppppyyy......')
        time.sleep(2)
        print('SPLASH!')
        time.sleep(2)
        print('What is that triangle in the water?')
        time.sleep(2)
        print('CHOMP!!')
        self.kill()
```

This relies on the kill() method we planned a while ago – so let's modify that to let us come back to life. If they choose to do so, we can use *not in* to have a list of rooms we don't want the player to end up in. We can then set the room and resuscitate them.

```python
def kill(self):
    self.alive = False
    print('Oh no. You appear to be dead!')
    anotherGo = input('Want another go? (y/n)').upper()
    if anotherGo == 'Y':
        print('You magically un-ghost. I wonder where your body will end up?')
        roomNumber = -1
        while roomNumber not in [23,9]:
            roomNumber = random.randint(1,23)
        self.setRoom(12)
        self.resuscitate()
    else:
```

```
            self.game.flipPlayStatus(
```

If they choose not to have another go, then we flip the game status to end the game.

```
Adding rooms
Adding long descriptions
running the game
tick
What do you want to do? move east

You move.

This is the rudder, the bit that turns the ship left and right. Mainly left
- probably because of the amount of rum consumed. It's... quite slippy...
Exits: None!
In fact... it is *really* slippy here!
A bit ... tooo.... slipppppyyy......
SPLASH!
What is that triangle in the water?
CHOMP!!
Oh no. You appear to be dead!
Want another go? (y/n)y
tick
What do you want to do? look
The starboard aft deck is just behind the main mast, towards the middle of t
he ship. There's quite a lot of deck cargo around - must be quite hard to mo
ve on this ship.
Exits: NORTH, SOUTH, DOWN
tick
What do you want to do?
```

Now how about that hammer? For this we will need to edit the *useItem()* method. Depending on how complex your game gets, you may have a whole bunch of options in here, with many nested if..elif..else statements. Here we can use the first if to test if they don't have an item they are trying to use:

```python
if not self.hasItem(item):
    print('You do not have a',item.lower())
```

```
Adding rooms
Adding long descriptions
running the game
tick
What do you want to do? use hammer
You do not have a hammer
tick
What do you want to do?
```

The final *else* is for trying to use something they **have** got – but has not been dealt with by any other methods. Here I have added a belaying-pin;

```python
#Else is using something you have, but it does nothing.
else:
    print('You think about using a',item.lower(),'but this does not seem like the right kind of place to do so.')
```

```
Adding rooms
Adding long descriptions
running the game
tick
What do you want to do? look
The poop deck (hahaha!) is the rearmost part of the ship, where the steering wheel is located. Posh people only up there!
A hammer is here.
A anvil is here.
A belaying-pin is here.
Exits: DOWN, EAST
tick
What do you want to do? get belaying-pin
You manage to get a belaying-pin
tick
What do you want to do? use belaying-pin
You think about using a belaying-pin but this does not seem like the right kind of place to do so.
tick
What do you want to do?
```

The elif's can be used for checking against specific situations. In this case, we will remove the wall (by adding the exits and changing the description for rooms 8 and 9.

But before we get there, let's think about a few things:
- Getting to room 9 to test this is a pain. Let's add a 'cheat' command to move us to a given room.

```python
def doCommand(self,verb,noun):
    if verb == 'HELP':
        self.help()
    elif verb == 'LOOK':
        if noun == None:
            self.look()
        else:
            self.lookItem(noun)
    elif verb == 'MOVE':
        self.move(noun)
    elif verb == 'GET':
        self.getItem(noun)
    elif verb == 'DROP':
        self.dropItem(noun)
    elif verb == 'USE':
        self.useItem(noun)
    elif verb == 'CHEAT':
        self.room = int(noun)
    else:
        print('Unknown verb or noun...')
```

now when we go to room 9, it's not very obvious that there's a challenge here! Maybe we should edit that description in CREATE.py a bit...

"The port midships is the port side of the middle of the ship. The foremast and mainast stretch way, way, way above you. There doesn't seem to be any way out! The North wall does look a bit weak, however... maybe it could be based down with something heavy?"

That's a bit more interesting! To add the exit, we need to update the addExit() method in ROOM.py to update the dictionary of exits.

```python
#This allows us to add a new exit direction which points to the ID of
whatever room we wish
def addExit(self,exitDirection,exitID):
    self.exits.update({exitDirection:exitID})
```

Then we just have to update the exits and the descriptions for rooms 8 and 9.

```python
elif item == "HAMMER" and self.getRoom() == 9:
    print('hurrah!')
    room = self.game.getRoom(self.getRoom())
    if room.getExits() == {}:
```

```python
            print('You bash away at the wall with your hammer')
            time.sleep(2)
            print('The wall comes down!')
            room.addExit('NORTH',8)
            room.setLongDesc("The port midships is the port side of the middle of the ship. The foremast and mainast stretch way, way, way above you. A rough hole has been based in the North wall.")
            room = self.game.getRoom(8)
            room.addExit('SOUTH',9)
            room.setLongDesc("The starboard midships is the starboard side of the middle of the ship, smack between the main mast and the foremast. Just ripe for anything falling from the masts to land on your noggin. A rough hole has been bashed in the South wall.")
```

```
Adding rooms
Adding long descriptions
running the game
tick
What do you want to do? get hammer
You manage to get a hammer
tick
What do you want to do? cheat 9
tick
What do you want to do? look
The port midships is the port side of the middle of the ship. The foremast and mainast stretch way, way, way above you. There doesn't seem to be any way out! The North wall does look a bit weak, however... maybe it could be based down with something heavy?
Exits:
tick
What do you want to do? use hammer
hurrah!
You bash away at the wall with your hammer
The wall comes down!
tick
What do you want to do? look
The port midships is the port side of the middle of the ship. The foremast and mainast stretch way, way, way above you. A rough hole has been based in the North wall.
Exits: NORTH
tick
What do you want to do? move north

You move.

The starboard midships is the starboard side of the middle of the ship, smack between the main mast and the foremast. Just ripe for anything falling from the masts to land on your noggin. A rough hole has been bashed in the South wall.
Exits: NORTH, SOUTH
tick
What do you want to do? look
The starboard midships is the starboard side of the middle of the ship, smack between the main mast and the foremast. Just ripe for anything falling from the masts to land on your noggin. A rough hole has been bashed in the South wall.
Exits: NORTH, SOUTH
tick
What do you want to do?
```

Let's think about that distractor. We need a knife – we can leave that in room 5 and create it in CREATE.py. We can add our sacks as well, though make them ungettable.

```
knife = Thing(4,'knife',"A really sharp knife, the kind sailors hold
between their teeth when swinging from ropes to help them go
OOOoooarrrrr properly.")
game.addItem(5,knife)
sacks = Thing(5,'sacks',"Bulging sacks. How interesting - I wonder what
is in them...",False)
game.addItem(12,sacks)
```

This time we will allow the knife to work anywhere where sacks are. You could even randomise the location! Then we just add an elif to useItem() to test if sacks are in the same area when we use the knife, and if so then we change the short and long descriptions of the sacks.

```
elif item == "KNIFE" and
self.game.getRoom(self.getRoom()).ifContains('SACKS'):
    thing = self.game.getRoom(self.getRoom()).ifContains('SACKS')
    print("The sacks disintegrate into scraps. There was nothing in them
after all!")
    thing.setShortDesc("scraps")
    thing.setLongDesc("scraps of cloth that may once have been sacks.")
```

Win the Game

Finally, we have puzzles to solve and distractors to… distract… the player. Now we just need to be able to win the game. How about we have the player enter room 1… but they *must* be holding a gold coin that they found when they went into the blocked off room (room 9).

Let's add the bling to CREATE.py:

```
coin = Thing(6,'coin',"A lovely blingy gold coin! With this in your
pocket and the right opportunity you just feel sure you could get off
this boat!")
game.addItem(9,coin)
```

And then we can edit *move()* in PLAYER.py to test whether the user is in room 1, and either output a message (if they don't have the coin) or let them win the game. We can add an *elif* after the *if* statement that tests if we are in room 1:

```
elif self.room == 1:
    if self.hasItem("COIN"):
        print('You ponder')
```

```python
        time.sleep(2)
        print('You reach into your pocket and pull out the golden coin.')
        time.sleep(2)
        print('You flick the coin in the air and... WHIZZZZZZ!')
        time.sleep(2)
        print('You find yourself teleported to the nicest of pirate islands, surrounded by gold and rum and ... gold...')
        time.sleep(2)
        print('YOU WIN! Well done :)')
        self.game.flipPlayStatus()
    else:
        print("This feels like a really opportune kind of place. You're just sure that with a little money in your pocket you could really make something of yourself from here.")
```

And that, as they say, is that! The game is now playable!

Some Final Tweaks

There are just a few things we need to go back and tweak to make ourselves as happy as pie. There are a few methods we didn't end up using – they all have the word *pass* in them – so we can go and delete them. Unless you want to implement them of course!

It's really frustrating that we can look at items in a room, but not that we are holding. So we should probably add an ITEMS command to *doCommand()*:

```python
elif verb == 'ITEMS':
    self.items()
```

And implement it:
```python
def listItems(self):
    count = 0
    print('Things you are holding:')
    for item in self.items:
        print('-',item.getShortDesc())
        count += 1
    if count == 0:
        print('- Nothing!')
```

And then alter the *lookItem()* method.

```python
def lookItem(self,noun):
    found = False
    room = self.game.getRoom(self.getRoom())
```

```
thing = room.ifContains(noun)
if thing != None:
    print(thing.getLongDesc())
    found = True
thing = self.hasItem(noun)
if thing != None:
    print(thing.getLongDesc())
    found = True
if not found:
    print('I cannot find one of them!')
```

Of course, after all this time we've not been updating HELP!

```
def help(self):
    print('Commands:')
    print('LOOK: Look around the current room.')
    print('LOOK <item>: Looks at a specified item.')
    print('MOVE <direction>: Move in the given direction')
    print('GET <item>: Tries to pick up an item.')
    print('DROP <item>: Tries to drop an item.')
    print('USE <item>: Tries to use an item.')
    print('ITEMS: Lists the items you are carrying.')
```

Of course, we chose not to include the CHEAT command in there!

You have written and edited a *lot* of code int his book. Final complete code can be found for checking in Appendix 2.

Appendix 1

WARNING: These files are for reference only. Some longer lines may wrap around – particularly comments. Be careful if you are typing them in!

Program the Game Map – Files

ROOM.py

```python
#An initial definition of a room
class Room:
    #Initialisation happens when you take this description and make it into
    #an object.
    # - self - all class definitions need this so that it can look at it's own properties & methods
    # - id - we will give it a number to identify itt by
    # - shortDesc will be the 'name' of the room
    # - exits will be a list of exits from the room
    # - contains will be a list of the things contained in the room
    # - longDesc will be the longer description which we will only see if we actually look around.
    #   as this is not strictly neccesary, we start it as nothing and then set it later if we
    #   so wish.
    def __init__(self, id, shortDesc, exits, contains):
        self.id = id
        self.shortDesc = shortDesc
        self.exits = exits
        self.contains = contains
        self.longDesc = ''

    #This will look at itself and give us back the ID
    def getId(self):
        return self.id #just give back whatever the ID is


    #This will look at itself and give us back the short description
    def getShortDesc(self):
        return self.shortDesc #just give back whatever the current short description is

    #This will take the new description we give it and set this as the object's short description
    def setShortDesc(self,desc):
        self.shortDesc = desc

    #This will look at itself and give us back the long description
    def getLongDesc(self):
        pass
```

```python
    #This will take the new description we give it and set this as the object's long description
    def setLongDesc(self,desc):
        self.longDesc = desc

    #This give us a list of exits
    def getExits(self):
        pass

    #This allows us to test if exit exists in our list of known exits
    def checkExitExists(self,exit):
        pass

    #This allows us to add a new exit direction which points to the ID of whatever room we wish
    def addExit(self,exitDirection,exitID):
        pass

    #This allows us to remove an exit
    def removeExit(self,exitDirection):
        pass

    #This will give us a list of things the room contains
    def getContains(self):
        pass

    #This will let us test if a particular item is in the room
    def ifContains(self,contains):
        pass

    #This lets us rmove an item from the room
    def remove(self,item):
        pass

    #This lets us put an item in to the room
    def putIn(self,item):
        pass
```

GAME.py

```python
#An initial definition of the game
class Game:
    #Initiaslisation happens when you take this description and make it into
    #an object.
    # - self - all class definitions need this so that it can look at it's own properties & methods
    # - rooms will be the dictionary of rooms - these will start as empty
    # - items will be the dictionary of items not held in a room - these will start as empty
    def __init__(self):
        self.rooms = {} #empty list
        self.items = {} #empty list
        self.status = False #not in play

    #This will tell us whether we are in play or not
    def getPlayStatus(self):
        return self.status

    #This will invert the play status (if we are playing, make us not playing and vice versa)
    def flipPlayStatus(self):
        self.status = not self.status

    #This will add an object to the items dictionary
    def addItem(self,item):
        pass

    #This will move an item to a room from the holding list
    def moveItemToRoom(self,itemId,roomId):
        pass

    #This will move an item from a room to the holding list
    def moveItemToRoom(self,itemId,roomId):
        pass

    #This will add a room to the rooms list
    #It stores it under it's own ID for ease of access
    def addRoom(self,room):
        self.rooms[room.getId()] = room

    #This will list all rooms currently 'owned' by the game
    # not useful for the player, but good for our debugging.
    def listRooms(self):
        print('Listing rooms')
        print('=============')
        for id in self.rooms:
            print(id, '->', self.rooms[id].getShortDesc())
```

```python
main.py (version 1)
#import the classes we have written
from GAME import Game
from ROOM import Room

#Create (instantiate) an instance of Game, called game
game = Game()

#Test the game status and that we can flip it
print('Is the game running?')
print(game.getPlayStatus())
print('Flip it around!')
game.flipPlayStatus()
print('Is the game running now?')
print(game.getPlayStatus())

#Create a room (we used room 1 for an example, and it currently does not
# contain anything)
room = Room(1,'Startboard Bows',None,None)
#Look at the room's short description
print(room.getShortDesc())

#Whoops - we made a typo! Change the short description and look again
room.setShortDesc('Starboard Bows')
print(room.getShortDesc())


main.py (version 2)
#import the classes we have written
from GAME import Game
from ROOM import Room

#Create (instantiate) an instance of Game, called game
game = Game()

#Create a room (we used room 1 for an example, and it currently does not
# contain anything)
room = Room(1,'Starboard Bows',None,None)

#Add the room to the game
print('Adding room 1')
game.addRoom(room)
game.listRooms()

#We can actually combine this into a single line:
print()
print('Adding room 2')
game.addRoom(Room(2,'Port Bows',None,None))
game.listRooms()
```

main.py (version 3)

```python
#import the classes we have written
from GAME import Game
from ROOM import Room

#Create (instantiate) an instance of Game, called game
game = Game()

print('Adding rooms')
game.addRoom(Room(1,'Starboard Bows',None,None))
game.addRoom(Room(2,'Port Bows',None,None))
game.addRoom(Room(3,'Starboard Forebeam',None,None))
game.addRoom(Room(4,'Starboard Foredeck',None,None))
game.addRoom(Room(5,'Port Foredeck',None,None))
game.addRoom(Room(6,'Port Forebeam',None,None))
game.addRoom(Room(7,'Starboard Beam',None,None))
game.addRoom(Room(8,'Starboard Midships',None,None))
game.addRoom(Room(9,'Port Midships',None,None))
game.addRoom(Room(10,'Port Beam',None,None))
game.addRoom(Room(11,'Starboard Quarter',None,None))
game.addRoom(Room(12,'Starboard Aft Deck',None,None))
game.addRoom(Room(13,'Port Aft Deck',None,None))
game.addRoom(Room(14,'Port Quarter',None,None))
game.addRoom(Room(15,'Poop Deck',None,None))
game.addRoom(Room(16,'Starboard Forecastle',None,None))
game.addRoom(Room(17,'Port Forecastle',None,None))
game.addRoom(Room(18,'Starboard Fore Hold',None,None))
game.addRoom(Room(19,'Port Fore Hold',None,None))
game.addRoom(Room(20,'Starboard Aft Hold',None,None))
game.addRoom(Room(21,'Port Aft Hold',None,None))
game.addRoom(Room(22,'Captain\'s Cabin',None,None))
game.addRoom(Room(23,'Rudder',None,None))

game.listRooms()
```

Tidy Up

ROOM.py
```python
#An initial definition of a room
class Room:
    #Initiiaslisation happens when you take this description and make it into
    #an object.
    # - self - all class definitions need this so that it can look at it's own properties & methods
    # - id - we will give it a number to identify itt by
    # - shortDesc will be the 'name' of the room
    # - exits will be a list of exits from the room
    # - contains will be a list of the things contained in the room
```

```python
    # - longDesc will be the longer description which we will only see if we actually look around.
    #    as this is not strictly neccesary, we start it as nothing and then set it later if we
    #    so wish.
    def __init__(self, id, shortDesc, exits, contains):
        self.id = id
        self.shortDesc = shortDesc
        self.exits = exits
        self.contains = contains
        self.longDesc = ''

    #This will look at itself and give us back the ID
    def getId(self):
        return self.id #just give back whatever the ID is


    #This will look at itself and give us back the short description
    def getShortDesc(self):
        return self.shortDesc #just give back whatever the current short description is

    #This will take the new description we give it and set this as the object's short description
    def setShortDesc(self,desc):
        self.shortDesc = desc

    #This will look at itself and give us back the long description
    def getLongDesc(self):
        return self.longDesc #Just give back whatever the current long desc is

    #This will take the new description we give it and set this as the object's long description
    def setLongDesc(self,desc):
        self.longDesc = desc

    #This give us a list of exits
    def getExits(self):
        pass

    #This allows us to test if exit exists in our list of known exits
    def checkExitExists(self,exit):
        pass

    #This allows us to add a new exit direction which points to the ID of whatever room we wish
    def addExit(self,exitDirection,exitID):
        pass
```

```python
    #This allows us to remove an exit
    def removeExit(self,exitDirection):
        pass

    #This will give us a list of things the room contains
    def getContains(self):
        pass

    #This will let us test if a particular item is in the room
    def ifContains(self,contains):
        pass

    #This lets us rmove an item from the room
    def remove(self,item):
        pass

    #This lets us put an item in to the room
    def putIn(self,item):
        pass
```

GAME.py

```python
#An initial definition of the game
class Game:
    #Initiaslisation happens when you take this description and make it into
    #an object.
    # - self - all class definitions need this so that it can look at it's own properties & methods
    # - rooms will be the dictionary of rooms - these will start as empty
    # - items will be the dictionary of items not held in a room - these will start as empty
    def __init__(self):
        self.rooms = {} #empty list
        self.items = {} #empty list
        self.status = False #not in play

    #This will tell us whether we are in play or not
    def getPlayStatus(self):
        return self.status

    #This will invert the play status (if we are playing, make us not playing and vice versa)
    def flipPlayStatus(self):
        self.status = not self.status

    #This will add an object to the items dictionary
    def addItem(self,item):
        pass
```

```python
    #This will move an item to a room from the holding list
    def moveItemToRoom(self,itemId,roomId):
        pass

    #This will move an item from a room to the holding list
    def moveItemToRoom(self,itemId,roomId):
        pass

    #This will add a room to the rooms list
    #It stores it under it's own ID for ease of access
    def addRoom(self,room):
        self.rooms[room.getId()] = room

    #This will list all rooms currently 'owned' by the game
    # not useful for the player, but good for our debugging.
    def listRooms(self):
        print('Listing rooms')
        print('==============')
        for id in self.rooms:
            print(id, '->', self.rooms[id].getShortDesc())

    #This will add a long description to a given room
    def addRoomLongDescription(self,room,desc):
        self.rooms[room].setLongDesc(desc)
```

CREATE.py
```python
from ROOM import Room
def Create(game):
 print('Adding rooms')
 game.addRoom(Room(1,'Starboard Bows',None,None))
 game.addRoom(Room(2,'Port Bows',None,None))
 game.addRoom(Room(3,'Starboard Forebeam',None,None))
 game.addRoom(Room(4,'Starboard Foredeck',None,None))
 game.addRoom(Room(5,'Port Foredeck',None,None))
 game.addRoom(Room(6,'Port Forebeam',None,None))
 game.addRoom(Room(7,'Starboard Beam',None,None))
 game.addRoom(Room(8,'Starboard Midships',None,None))
 game.addRoom(Room(9,'Port Midships',None,None))
 game.addRoom(Room(10,'Port Beam',None,None))
 game.addRoom(Room(11,'Starboard Quarter',None,None))
 game.addRoom(Room(12,'Starboard Aft Deck',None,None))
 game.addRoom(Room(13,'Port Aft Deck',None,None))
 game.addRoom(Room(14,'Port Quarter',None,None))
 game.addRoom(Room(15,'Poop Deck',None,None))
 game.addRoom(Room(16,'Starboard Forecastle',None,None))
 game.addRoom(Room(17,'Port Forecastle',None,None))
 game.addRoom(Room(18,'Starboard Fore Hold',None,None))
 game.addRoom(Room(19,'Port Fore Hold',None,None))
 game.addRoom(Room(20,'Starboard Aft Hold',None,None))
 game.addRoom(Room(21,'Port Aft Hold',None,None))
```

```python
game.addRoom(Room(22,'Captain\'s Cabin',None,None))
game.addRoom(Room(23,'Rudder',None,None))

print('Adding long descriptions')
game.addRoomLongDescription(1,"This is the starboard bow of the good ship Nautilus. You can see the bowsprit point forwards and the rest of the ship is to the rear, on account of this being the front. There is a lot of sea about, isn't there?")
game.addRoomLongDescription(2,"This is the port bow of the good ship Nautilus. You can see the bowsprit point forwards and the rest of the ship is to the rear, on account of this being the front. The starboard bow is just over there. There is a lot of sea about, isn't there?")
game.addRoomLongDescription(3,"The starboard forebeam is the little bit of deck just forward of the starboard beam and just abeam of the starboard foredeck. It's main reason to exist is because ships don't really divide into nice even shapes.")
game.addRoomLongDescription(4,"The starboard foredeck is just ahead of the foremast and as far forward as you can get without looking like Leonardo Di Caprio")
game.addRoomLongDescription(5,"The port foredeck is just ahead of the foremast. If you go any further forward you might find yourself doing impressions of Claire Danes")
game.addRoomLongDescription(6,"The port forebeam is the little bit of deck just like the starboard forebeam, only the other way around.")
game.addRoomLongDescription(7,"The starboard beam is half way down the starboard side of the ship, overlooking the deep, deep sea.")
game.addRoomLongDescription(8,"The starboard midships is the starboard side of the middle of the ship, smack between the main mast and the foremast. Just ripe for anything falling from the masts to land on your noggin.")
game.addRoomLongDescription(9,"The port midships is the port side of the middle of the ship. The foremast and mainast stretch way, way, way above you.")
game.addRoomLongDescription(10,"The port beam is half way down the port side of the ship, overlooking the deep, deep sea. In fact, when the ship rolls just so, it's overhanging... the... sea. Gulp!")
game.addRoomLongDescription(11,"The starboard quarter is the almost all the way to the back, and on the starboard side, of the Nautilus. Any further aft and you'd be on the poop deck.")
game.addRoomLongDescription(12,"The starboard aft deck is just behind the main mast, towards the middle of the ship. There's quite a lot of deck cargo around - must be quite hard to move on this ship.")
game.addRoomLongDescription(13,"The port aft deck is just behind the main mast, towards the middle of the ship, just opposite the starboard aft deck. There's quite a lot of deck cargo around - must be quite hard to move on this ship.")
game.addRoomLongDescription(14,"The port quarter is the almost all the way to the back, and on the port side, of the Nautilus. You can't half feel the roll of the ship from here!")
```

```python
    game.addRoomLongDescription(15,"The poop deck (hahaha!) is the rearmost part of the ship, where the steering wheel is located. Posh people only up there!")
    game.addRoomLongDescription(16,"The forecastle is where the ropes - and rats - hang out. It's small, cramped, and quite smelly!")
    game.addRoomLongDescription(17,"The forecastle is where the ropes - and rats - hang out. It's small, cramped, and quite smelly!")
    game.addRoomLongDescription(18,"The forehold is where quite a lot of the cargo is kept, and split into two halves. This side looks like mainly wool - not the kind of loot you'd expect from a good pirate!")
    game.addRoomLongDescription(19,"The forehold is where quite a lot of the cargo is kept, and split into two halves. This side looks like mainly barrels of rum - which explains why the ship keeps sailing in circles...")
    game.addRoomLongDescription(20,"The aft hold is slightly longer than the forehold. This part seems to be mainly spare parts - old sails, sticks (or are they masts) and that kind of thing. It's quite cramped!")
    game.addRoomLongDescription(21,"The aft hold is slightly longer than the forehold. This part seems to be mainly paintings of the Captain's wife. How very odd!")
    game.addRoomLongDescription(22,"The captain's cabin stretches the whole width of the ship and is filled with a nice dining table, a cot, and some books. As it's a pirate ship the books are mainly of the type that involve cats sitting in hats.")
    game.addRoomLongDescription(23,"This is the rudder, the bit that turns the ship left and right. Mainly left - probably because of the amount of rum consumed. It's... quite slippy...")
    game.listRooms()
```

main.py (version 4)
```python
#import the classes we have written
from GAME import Game
from ROOM import Room
from CREATE import Create
#Create (instantiate) an instance of Game, called game
game = Game()
Create(game)
```

Add Exits

CREATE.py
```python
from ROOM import Room
def Create(game):
    print('Adding rooms')
    game.addRoom(Room(1,'Starboard Bows',{"DOWN":16,"SOUTH":2},None))
    game.addRoom(Room(2,'Port Bows',{"NORTH":1},None))
    game.addRoom(Room(3,'Starboard Forebeam',{"DOWN":18,"SOUTH":4},None))
    game.addRoom(Room(4,'Starboard Foredeck',{"NORTH":3,"SOUTH":5},None))
    game.addRoom(Room(5,'Port Foredeck',{"NORTH":4,"SOUTH":6},None))
```

```python
  game.addRoom(Room(6,'Port Forebeam',{"NORTH":5,"EAST":10},None))
  game.addRoom(Room(7,'Starboard Beam',{"EAST":11,"SOUTH":8},None))
  game.addRoom(Room(8,'Starboard Midships',{"NORTH":7},None))
  game.addRoom(Room(9,'Port Midships',{},None))
  game.addRoom(Room(10,'Port Beam',{"NORTH":9,"EAST":14,"WEST":6},None))
  game.addRoom(Room(11,'Starboard Quarter',{"SOUTH":12,"WEST":7},None))
  game.addRoom(Room(12,'Starboard Aft Deck',{"NORTH":11,"SOUTH":13,"DOWN":20},None))
  game.addRoom(Room(13,'Port Aft Deck',{"NORTH":12,"SOUTH":14},None))
  game.addRoom(Room(14,'Port Quarter',{"NORTH":13,"WEST":10},None))
  game.addRoom(Room(15,'Poop Deck',{"DOWN":22,"EAST":23},None))
  game.addRoom(Room(16,'Starboard Forecastle',{"UP":1,"SOUTH":17},None))
  game.addRoom(Room(17,'Port Forecastle',{"NORTH":16,"EAST":19},None))
  game.addRoom(Room(18,'Starboard Fore Hold',{"UP":13,"EAST":20,"SOUTH":19},None))
  game.addRoom(Room(19,'Port Fore Hold',{"NORTH":18,"WEST":17},None))
  game.addRoom(Room(20,'Starboard Aft Hold',{"UP":12,"SOUTH":21},None))
  game.addRoom(Room(21,'Port Aft Hold',{"NORTH":20,"EAST":22},None))
  game.addRoom(Room(22,'Captain\'s Cabin',{"UP":15,"WEST":21},None))
  game.addRoom(Room(23,'Rudder',None,None))

  print('Adding long descriptions')
  game.addRoomLongDescription(1,"This is the starboard bow of the good ship Nautilus. You can see the bowsprit point forwards and the rest of the ship is to the rear, on account of this being the front. There is a lot of sea about, isn't there?")
  game.addRoomLongDescription(2,"This is the port bow of the good ship Nautilus. You can see the bowsprit point forwards and the rest of the ship is to the rear, on account of this being the front. The starboard bow is just over there. There is a lot of sea about, isn't there?")
  game.addRoomLongDescription(3,"The starboard forebeam is the little bit of deck just forward of the starboard beam and just abeam of the starboard foredeck. It's main reason to exist is because ships don't really divide into nice even shapes.")
  game.addRoomLongDescription(4,"The starboard foredeck is just ahead of the foremast and as far forward as you can get without looking like Leonardo Di Caprio")
  game.addRoomLongDescription(5,"The port foredeck is just ahead of the foremast. If you go any further forward you might find yourself doing impressions of Claire Danes")
  game.addRoomLongDescription(6,"The port forebeam is the little bit of deck just like the starboard forebeam, only the other way around.")
  game.addRoomLongDescription(7,"The starboard beam is half way down the starboard side of the ship, overlooking the deep, deep sea.")
  game.addRoomLongDescription(8,"The starboard midships is the starboard side of the middle of the ship, smack between the main mast and the foremast. Just ripe for anything falling from the masts to land on your noggin.")
```

```
    game.addRoomLongDescription(9,"The port midships is the port side of
the middle of the ship. The foremast and mainast stretch way, way, way
above you.")
    game.addRoomLongDescription(10,"The port beam is half way down the
port side of the ship, overlooking the deep, deep sea. In fact, when the
ship rolls just so, it's overhanging... the... sea. Gulp!")
    game.addRoomLongDescription(11,"The starboard quarter is the almost
all the way to the back, and on the starboard side, of the Nautilus. Any
further aft and you'd be on the poop deck.")
    game.addRoomLongDescription(12,"The starboard aft deck is just behind
the main mast, towards the middle of the ship. There's quite a lot of
deck cargo around - must be quite hard to move on this ship.")
    game.addRoomLongDescription(13,"The port aft deck is just behind the
main mast, towards the middle of the ship, just opposite the starboard
aft deck. There's quite a lot of deck cargo around - must be quite hard
to move on this ship.")
    game.addRoomLongDescription(14,"The port quarter is the almost all the
way to the back, and on the port side, of the Nautilus. You can't half
feel the roll of the ship from here!")
    game.addRoomLongDescription(15,"The poop deck (hahaha!) is the
rearmost part of the ship, where the steering wheel is located. Posh
people only up there!")
    game.addRoomLongDescription(16,"The forecastle is where the ropes -
and rats - hang out. It's small, cramped, and quite smelly!")
    game.addRoomLongDescription(17,"The forecastle is where the ropes -
and rats - hang out. It's small, cramped, and quite smelly!")
    game.addRoomLongDescription(18,"The forehold is where quite a lot of
the cargo is kept, and split into two halves. This side looks like
mainly wool - not the kind of loot you'd expect from a good pirate!")
    game.addRoomLongDescription(19,"The forehold is where quite a lot of
the cargo is kept, and split into two halves. This side looks like
mainly barrels of rum - which explains why the ship keeps sailing in
circles...")
    game.addRoomLongDescription(20,"The aft hold is slightly longer than
the forehold. This part seems to be mainly spare parts - old sails,
sticks (or are they masts) and that kind of thing. It's quite cramped!")
    game.addRoomLongDescription(21,"The aft hold is slightly longer than
the forehold. This part seems to be mainly paintings of the Captain's
wife. How very odd!")
    game.addRoomLongDescription(22,"The captain's cabin stretches the
whole width of the ship and is filled with a nice dining table, a cot,
and some books. As it's a pirate ship the books are mainly of the type
that involve cats sitting in hats.")
    game.addRoomLongDescription(23,"This is the rudder, the bit that turns
the ship left and right. Mainly left - probably because of the amount of
rum consumed. It's... quite slippy...")
    #game.listRooms()
```

Program a player

PLAYER.py

```python
#An initial definition of a player
class Player:
    #Initialisation happens when you take this description and make it into
    #an object.
    # - self - all class definitions need this so that it can look at it's own properties & methods
    def __init__(self):
        self.alive = True
        self.room = None
        self.items = {}
        self.game = None

    def setGame(self,game):
        self.game = game

    def isAlive(self):
        return self.alive

    def kill(self):
        self.alive = False

    def resuscitate(self):
        self.alive = True

    def setRoom(self,room):
        self.room = room

    def getRoom(self):
        return self.room

    def look(self):
        room = self.game.getRoom(self.getRoom())
        print(room.getLongDesc())
        #print(room.getExits())
        exits = room.getExits()
        keys = ', '.join(exits.keys())
        print('Exits: '+keys)

    def getItem(self,item):
        pass

    def dropItem(self,item):
        pass

    def useItem(self,item):
        pass
```

```python
    def move(self,direction):
        room = self.game.getRoom(self.getRoom())
        exits = room.getExits()
        if direction in exits.keys():
            print('\nYou move.\n')
            self.room = exits[direction]
            self.look()
        else:
            print('I cannot move that way')

    def doCommand(self,verb,noun):
        if verb == 'HELP':
            self.help()
        elif verb == 'LOOK':
            self.look()
        elif verb == 'MOVE':
            self.move(noun)
        else:
            print('Unknown verb or noun...')

    def help(self):
        print('Commands:')
        print('LOOK: Look around the current room.')
        print('MOVE <direction>: Move in the given direction')

    def getCommand(self):
        command = input('What do you want to do? ').upper()
        commands = command.split(' ')
        while True:
            if len(commands) == 1:
                verb = commands[0]
                self.doCommand(verb,None)
                break
            elif len(commands) == 2:
                verb = commands[0]
                noun = commands[1]
                self.doCommand(verb,noun)
                break
            else:
                print('Please enter a verb followed by an optional noun.')
                print('Enter HELP for help.')
```

Updated main.py
```
#import the classes we have written
from GAME import Game
from ROOM import Room
from CREATE import Create
from PLAYER import Player
```

```python
#Create (instantiate) an instance of Game, called game
game = Game()
Create(game)

#Create (instantiate) a Player called player
player = Player()
player.setRoom(15)
player.setGame(game)
game.addPlayer(player)

#Run the game
print('running the game')
game.flipPlayStatus()
while game.getPlayStatus():
    game.tick()

print('game ended')
```

Program some Things

THING.py

```python
#An initial definition of a thing
class Thing:
    def __init__(self, id, shortDesc, longDesc, gettable = True):
        self.id = id
        self.shortDesc = shortDesc
        self.longDesc = longDesc
        self.gettable = gettable

    #This will look at itself and give us back the ID
    def getId(self):
        return self.id #just give back whatever the ID is

    #This will look at itself and give us back the short description
    def getShortDesc(self):
        return self.shortDesc #just give back whatever the current short description is

    #This will take the new description we give it and set this as the object's short description
    def setShortDesc(self,desc):
        self.shortDesc = desc

    #This will look at itself and give us back the long description
    def getLongDesc(self):
        return self.longDesc #Just give back whatever the current long desc is
```

```python
    #This will take the new description we give it and set this as the object's long description
    def setLongDesc(self,desc):
        self.longDesc = desc

    #This will toggle the gettability of the thing
    def toggleGettable(self):
        self.gettable = not self.gettable

    #This will return weather a thing can be got
    def isGettable(self):
        return self.gettable
```

ROOM.py
```python
#An initial definition of a room
class Room:
    #Initiiaslisation happens when you take this description and make it into
    #an object.
    # - self - all class definitions need this so that it can look at it's own properties & methods
    # - id - we will give it a number to identify itt by
    # - shortDesc will be the 'name' of the room
    # - exits will be a list of exits from the room
    # - contains will be a list of the things contained in the room
    # - longDesc will be the longer description which we will only see if we actually look around.
    #   as this is not strictly neccesary, we start it as nothing and then set it later if we
    #   so wish.
    def __init__(self, id, shortDesc, exits, contains):
        self.id = id
        self.shortDesc = shortDesc
        self.exits = exits
        self.contains = contains
        self.longDesc = ''

    #This will look at itself and give us back the ID
    def getId(self):
        return self.id #just give back whatever the ID is


    #This will look at itself and give us back the short description
    def getShortDesc(self):
        return self.shortDesc #just give back whatever the current short description is

    #This will take the new description we give it and set this as the object's short description
    def setShortDesc(self,desc):
```

```python
        self.shortDesc = desc

    #This will look at itself and give us back the long description
    def getLongDesc(self):
        return self.longDesc #Just give back whatever the current long desc is

    #This will take the new description we give it and set this as the object's long description
    def setLongDesc(self,desc):
        self.longDesc = desc

    #This give us a list of exits
    def getExits(self):
        return self.exits

    #This allows us to test if exit exists in our list of known exits
    def checkExitExists(self,exit):
        pass

    #This allows us to add a new exit direction which points to the ID of whatever room we wish
    def addExit(self,exitDirection,exitID):
        pass

    #This allows us to remove an exit
    def removeExit(self,exitDirection):
        pass

    #This will give us a list of things the room contains
    def getContains(self):
        return self.contains

    #This will let us test if a particular item is in the room
    def ifContains(self,lookingFor):
        items = self.getContains()
        for item in items:
            if item.getShortDesc().upper() == lookingFor:
                return item
        return None

    #This lets us remove an item from the room
    def remove(self,item):
        self.contains.remove(item)

    #This lets us put an item in to the room
    def putIn(self,item):
        self.contains.append(item)
```

PLAYER.py
```python
#An initial definition of a player
class Player:
    #Initialisation happens when you take this description and make it into
    #an object.
    # - self - all class definitions need this so that it can look at it's own properties & methods
    def __init__(self):
        self.alive = True
        self.room = None
        self.items = [] #Changed to [] instead of {}
        self.game = None

    def setGame(self,game):
        self.game = game

    def isAlive(self):
        return self.alive

    def kill(self):
        self.alive = False

    def resuscitate(self):
        self.alive = True

    def setRoom(self,room):
        self.room = room

    def getRoom(self):
        return self.room

    def look(self):
        room = self.game.getRoom(self.getRoom())
        print(room.getLongDesc())
        for thing in room.getContains():
            print('A',thing.getShortDesc(),'is here.')
        exits = room.getExits()
        keys = ', '.join(exits.keys())
        print('Exits: '+keys)

    def lookItem(self,noun):
        room = self.game.getRoom(self.getRoom())
        thing = room.ifContains(noun)
        if thing != None:
            print(thing.getLongDesc())
        else:
            print('I cannot find one of them!')

    #This will let us test if a particular item is held
```

```python
    #It is very similar to the room code!
    def hasItem(self,lookingFor):
        items = self.items
        for item in items:
            if item.getShortDesc().upper() == lookingFor:
                return item
        return None

    def getItem(self,noun):
        room = self.game.getRoom(self.getRoom())
        thing = room.ifContains(noun)
        if thing != None:
            self.items.append(thing)
            room.remove(thing)
            print('You manage to get a',noun.lower())
            if not thing.isGettable():
                print('Uh-oh... you struggle to hold a',noun.lower())
                self.dropItem(noun)
        else:
            print('You cannot find a',noun.lower())

    def dropItem(self,noun):
        room = self.game.getRoom(self.getRoom())
        thing = self.hasItem(noun)
        if thing != None:
            room.putIn(thing)
            self.items.remove(thing)
            print('You drop a',noun.lower())
        else:
            print('You do not have a',noun.lower(),'to drop!')

    def useItem(self,item):
        print('You do not know how to use items. Yet!')

    def move(self,direction):
        room = self.game.getRoom(self.getRoom())
        exits = room.getExits()
        if direction in exits.keys():
            print('\nYou move.\n')
            self.room = exits[direction]
            self.look()
        else:
            print('I cannot move that way')

    def doCommand(self,verb,noun):
        if verb == 'HELP':
            self.help()
        elif verb == 'LOOK':
            if noun == None:
                self.look()
```

```python
            else:
                self.lookItem(noun)
        elif verb == 'MOVE':
            self.move(noun)
        elif verb == 'GET':
            self.getItem(noun)
        elif verb == 'DROP':
            self.dropItem(noun)
        elif verb == 'USE':
            self.useItem(noun)
        else:
            print('Unknown verb or noun...')

    def help(self):
        print('Commands:')
        print('LOOK: Look around the current room.')
        print('MOVE <direction>: Move in the given direction')

    def getCommand(self):
        command = input('What do you want to do? ').upper()
        commands = command.split(' ')
        while True:
            if len(commands) == 1:
                verb = commands[0]
                self.doCommand(verb,None)
                break
            elif len(commands) == 2:
                verb = commands[0]
                noun = commands[1]
                self.doCommand(verb,noun)
                break
            else:
                print('Please enter a verb followed by an optional noun.')
                print('Enter HELP for help.')
```

GAME.py
```python
#An initial definition of the game
class Game:
    #Initiaslisation happens when you take this description and make it into
    #an object.
    # - self - all class definitions need this so that it can look at it's own properties & methods
    # - rooms will be the dictionary of rooms - these will start as empty
    # - items will be the dictionary of items not held in a room - these will start as empty
    def __init__(self):
```

```python
        self.rooms = {} #empty list
        self.items = {} #empty list
        self.status = False #not in play
        self.player = None #No player until we add them

    #This will tell us whether we are in play or not
    def getPlayStatus(self):
        return self.status

    #This will invert the play status (if we are playing, make us not playing and vice versa)
    def flipPlayStatus(self):
        self.status = not self.status

    #This will add an object to the items dictionary
    def addItem(self,room,item):
        self.rooms[room].putIn(item)

    #This will add a room to the rooms list
    #It stores it under it's own ID for ease of access
    def addRoom(self,room):
        self.rooms[room.getId()] = room

    #This will list all rooms currently 'owned' by the game
    # not useful for the player, but good for our debugging.
    def listRooms(self):
        print('Listing rooms')
        print('==============')
        for id in self.rooms:
            print(id, '->', self.rooms[id].getShortDesc())

    #This will add a long description to a given room
    def addRoomLongDescription(self,room,desc):
        self.rooms[room].setLongDesc(desc)

    #This will add the player to the game
    def addPlayer(self,player):
        self.player = player

    #This will take an id, and return the room object with that id
    def getRoom(self,id):
        return self.rooms[id]

    #A 'tick' is a round of the game. The game does any
    #house keeping it may need and then gives the player
    #an opportunity to do it's thing.
    def tick(self):
        print('tick')
        self.player.getCommand()
```

Additional lines at the end of CREATE.py

```python
#Add some items
hammer = Thing(1,'hammer',"It's got a wooden handle and a heavy bit on the end. It's heavy enough to smash a wall down, or break your toe if you're not careful!")
game.addItem(15,hammer)
anvil = Thing(2,'anvil',"A huge piece of iron the sailors use when mending chain. Probably too big to move - it's a miracle the ship is still afloat really!",False)
game.addItem(15,anvil)
```

Appendix 2
Final Complete Code

main.py
```python
#import the classes we have written
from GAME import Game
from ROOM import Room
from CREATE import Create
from PLAYER import Player

#Create (instantiate) an instance of Game, called game
game = Game()
Create(game)

#Create (instantiate) a Player called player
player = Player()
player.setRoom(15)
player.setGame(game)
game.addPlayer(player)

#Run the game
print('running the game')
game.flipPlayStatus()
while game.getPlayStatus():
    game.tick()

print('game ended')
```

CREATE.py
```python
from ROOM import Room
from THING import Thing

def Create(game):
  print('Adding rooms')
  game.addRoom(Room(1,'Starboard Bows',{"DOWN":16,"SOUTH":2},[]))
  game.addRoom(Room(2,'Port Bows',{"NORTH":1},[]))
```

```python
    game.addRoom(Room(3,'Starboard Forebeam',{"DOWN":18,"SOUTH":4},[]))
    game.addRoom(Room(4,'Starboard Foredeck',{"NORTH":3,"SOUTH":5},[]))
    game.addRoom(Room(5,'Port Foredeck',{"NORTH":4,"SOUTH":6},[]))
    game.addRoom(Room(6,'Port Forebeam',{"NORTH":5,"EAST":10},[]))
    game.addRoom(Room(7,'Starboard Beam',{"EAST":11,"SOUTH":8},[]))
    game.addRoom(Room(8,'Starboard Midships',{"NORTH":7},[]))
    game.addRoom(Room(9,'Port Midships',{},[]))
    game.addRoom(Room(10,'Port Beam',{"NORTH":9,"EAST":14,"WEST":6},[]))
    game.addRoom(Room(11,'Starboard Quarter',{"SOUTH":12,"WEST":7},[]))
    game.addRoom(Room(12,'Starboard Aft Deck',{"NORTH":11,"SOUTH":13,"DOWN":20},[]))
    game.addRoom(Room(13,'Port Aft Deck',{"NORTH":12,"SOUTH":14},[]))
    game.addRoom(Room(14,'Port Quarter',{"NORTH":13,"WEST":10},[]))
    game.addRoom(Room(15,'Poop Deck',{"DOWN":22,"EAST":23},[]))
    game.addRoom(Room(16,'Starboard Forecastle',{"UP":1,"SOUTH":17},[]))
    game.addRoom(Room(17,'Port Forecastle',{"NORTH":16,"EAST":19},[]))
    game.addRoom(Room(18,'Starboard Fore Hold',{"UP":13,"EAST":20,"SOUTH":19},[]))
    game.addRoom(Room(19,'Port Fore Hold',{"NORTH":18,"WEST":17},[]))
    game.addRoom(Room(20,'Starboard Aft Hold',{"UP":12,"SOUTH":21},[]))
    game.addRoom(Room(21,'Port Aft Hold',{"NORTH":20,"EAST":22},[]))
    game.addRoom(Room(22,'Captain\'s Cabin',{"UP":15,"WEST":21},[]))
    game.addRoom(Room(23,'Rudder',None,[]))

    print('Adding long descriptions')
    game.addRoomLongDescription(1,"This is the starboard bow of the good ship Nautilus. You can see the bowsprit point forwards and the rest of the ship is to the rear, on account of this being the front. There is a lot of sea about, isn't there?")
    game.addRoomLongDescription(2,"This is the port bow of the good ship Nautilus. You can see the bowsprit point forwards and the rest of the ship is to the rear, on account of this being the front. The starboard bow is just over there. There is a lot of sea about, isn't there?")
    game.addRoomLongDescription(3,"The starboard forebeam is the little bit of deck just forward of the starboard beam and just abeam of the starboard foredeck. It's main reason to exist is because ships don't really divide into nice even shapes.")
    game.addRoomLongDescription(4,"The starboard foredeck is just ahead of the foremast and as far forward as you can get without looking like Leonardo Di Caprio")
    game.addRoomLongDescription(5,"The port foredeck is just ahead of the foremast. If you go any further forward you might find yourself doing impressions of Claire Danes")
    game.addRoomLongDescription(6,"The port forebeam is the little bit of deck just like the starboard forebeam, only the other way around.")
    game.addRoomLongDescription(7,"The starboard beam is half way down the starboard side of the ship, overlooking the deep, deep sea.")
    game.addRoomLongDescription(8,"The starboard midships is the starboard side of the middle of the ship, smack between the main mast and the
```

```
foremast. Just ripe for anything falling from the masts to land on your
noggin.")
    game.addRoomLongDescription(9,"The port midships is the port side of
the middle of the ship. The foremast and mainast stretch way, way, way
above you. There doesn't seem to be any way out! The North wall does
look a bit weak, however... maybe it could be based down with something
heavy?")
    game.addRoomLongDescription(10,"The port beam is half way down the
port side of the ship, overlooking the deep, deep sea. In fact, when the
ship rolls just so, it's overhanging... the... sea. Gulp!")
    game.addRoomLongDescription(11,"The starboard quarter is the almost
all the way to the back, and on the starboard side, of the Nautilus. Any
further aft and you'd be on the poop deck.")
    game.addRoomLongDescription(12,"The starboard aft deck is just behind
the main mast, towards the middle of the ship. There's quite a lot of
deck cargo around - must be quite hard to move on this ship.")
    game.addRoomLongDescription(13,"The port aft deck is just behind the
main mast, towards the middle of the ship, just opposite the starboard
aft deck. There's quite a lot of deck cargo around - must be quite hard
to move on this ship.")
    game.addRoomLongDescription(14,"The port quarter is the almost all the
way to the back, and on the port side, of the Nautilus. You can't half
feel the roll of the ship from here!")
    game.addRoomLongDescription(15,"The poop deck (hahaha!) is the
rearmost part of the ship, where the steering wheel is located. Posh
people only up there!")
    game.addRoomLongDescription(16,"The forecastle is where the ropes -
and rats - hang out. It's small, cramped, and quite smelly!")
    game.addRoomLongDescription(17,"The forecastle is where the ropes -
and rats - hang out. It's small, cramped, and quite smelly!")
    game.addRoomLongDescription(18,"The forehold is where quite a lot of
the cargo is kept, and split into two halves. This side looks like
mainly wool - not the kind of loot you'd expect from a good pirate!")
    game.addRoomLongDescription(19,"The forehold is where quite a lot of
the cargo is kept, and split into two halves. This side looks like
mainly barrels of rum - which explains why the ship keeps sailing in
circles...")
    game.addRoomLongDescription(20,"The aft hold is slightly longer than
the forehold. This part seems to be mainly spare parts - old sails,
sticks (or are they masts) and that kind of thing. It's quite cramped!")
    game.addRoomLongDescription(21,"The aft hold is slightly longer than
the forehold. This part seems to be mainly paintings of the Captain's
wife. How very odd!")
    game.addRoomLongDescription(22,"The captain's cabin stretches the
whole width of the ship and is filled with a nice dining table, a cot,
and some books. As it's a pirate ship the books are mainly of the type
that involve cats sitting in hats.")
    game.addRoomLongDescription(23,"This is the rudder, the bit that turns
the ship left and right. Mainly left - probably because of the amount of
rum consumed. It's... quite slippy...")
```

```python
    #game.listRooms()

    #Add some items
    hammer = Thing(1,'hammer',"It's got a wooden handle and a heavy bit on the end. It's heavy enough to smash a wall down, or break your toe if you're not careful!")
    game.addItem(15,hammer)
    anvil = Thing(2,'anvil',"A huge piece of iron the sailors use when mending chain. Probably too big to move - it's a miracle the ship is still afloat really!",False)
    game.addItem(15,anvil)
    pin = Thing(3,'belaying-pin',"A bit of wood for belaying ropes. Can you see any ropes that need belaying?")
    game.addItem(15,pin)
    knife = Thing(4,'knife',"A really sharp knife, the kind sailors hold between their teeth when swinging from ropes to help them go OOOoooarrrrr properly.")
    game.addItem(5,knife)
    sacks = Thing(5,'sacks',"Bulging sacks. How interesting - I wonder what is in them...",False)
    game.addItem(12,sacks)
    coin = Thing(6,'coin',"A lovely blingy gold coin! With this in your pocket and the right opportunity you just feel sure you could get off this boat!")
    game.addItem(9,coin)
```

GAME.py

```python
#An initial definition of the game
class Game:
    #Initiaslisation happens when you take this description and make it into
    #an object.
    # - self - all class definitions need this so that it can look at it's own properties & methods
    # - rooms will be the dictionary of rooms - these will start as empty
    # - items will be the dictionary of items not held in a room - these will start as empty
    def __init__(self):
        self.rooms = {} #empty list
        self.items = {} #empty list
        self.status = False #not in play
        self.player = None #No player until we add them

    #This will tell us whether we are in play or not
    def getPlayStatus(self):
        return self.status

    #This will invert the play status (if we are playing, make us not playing and vice versa)
```

```python
    def flipPlayStatus(self):
        self.status = not self.status

    #This will add an object to the items dictionary
    def addItem(self,room,item):
        self.rooms[room].putIn(item)

    #This will add a room to the rooms list
    #It stores it under it's own ID for ease of access
    def addRoom(self,room):
        self.rooms[room.getId()] = room

    #This will list all rooms currently 'owned' by the game
    # not useful for the player, but good for our debugging.
    def listRooms(self):
        print('Listing rooms')
        print('==============')
        for id in self.rooms:
            print(id, '->', self.rooms[id].getShortDesc())

    #This will add a long description to a given room
    def addRoomLongDescription(self,room,desc):
        self.rooms[room].setLongDesc(desc)

    #This will add the player to the game
    def addPlayer(self,player):
        self.player = player

    #This will take an id, and return the room object with that id
    def getRoom(self,id):
        return self.rooms[id]

    #A 'tick' is a round of the game. The game does any
    #house keeping it may need and then gives the player
    #an opportunity to do it's thing.
    def tick(self):
        print('tick')
        self.player.getCommand()
```

PLAYER.py

```python
import time
import random

#An initial definition of a player
class Player:
    #Initialisation happens when you take this description and make it into
    #an object.
    # - self - all class definitions need this so that it can look at it's own properties & methods
```

```python
    def __init__(self):
        self.alive = True
        self.room = None
        self.items = [] #Changed to [] instead of {}
        self.game = None

    def setGame(self,game):
        self.game = game

    def isAlive(self):
        return self.alive

    def kill(self):
        self.alive = False
        print('Oh no. You appear to be dead!')
        anotherGo = input('Want another go? (y/n)').upper()
        if anotherGo == 'Y':
            print('You magically un-ghost. I wonder where your body will end up?')
            roomNumber = -1
            while roomNumber not in [23,9]:
                roomNumber = random.randint(1,23)
            self.setRoom(12)
            self.resuscitate()
        else:
            self.game.flipPlayStatus()

    def resuscitate(self):
        self.alive = True

    def setRoom(self,room):
        self.room = room

    def getRoom(self):
        return self.room

    def look(self):
        room = self.game.getRoom(self.getRoom())
        print(room.getLongDesc())
        for thing in room.getContains():
            print('A',thing.getShortDesc(),'is here.')
        try:
            exits = room.getExits()
            keys = ', '.join(exits.keys())
        except:
            keys = "None!"
        print('Exits: '+keys)

    def lookItem(self,noun):
        found = False
```

```python
        room = self.game.getRoom(self.getRoom())
        thing = room.ifContains(noun)
        if thing != None:
            print(thing.getLongDesc())
            found = True
        thing = self.hasItem(noun)
        if thing != None:
            print(thing.getLongDesc())
            found = True
        if not found:
            print('I cannot find one of them!')

    #This will let us test if a particular item is held
    #It is very similar to the room code!
    def hasItem(self,lookingFor):
        items = self.items
        for item in items:
            if item.getShortDesc().upper() == lookingFor:
                return item
        return None

    def getItem(self,noun):
        room = self.game.getRoom(self.getRoom())
        thing = room.ifContains(noun)
        if thing != None:
            self.items.append(thing)
            room.remove(thing)
            print('You manage to get a',noun.lower())
            if not thing.isGettable():
                print('Uh-oh... you struggle to hold a',noun.lower())
                self.dropItem(noun)
        else:
            print('You cannot find a',noun.lower())

    def dropItem(self,noun):
        room = self.game.getRoom(self.getRoom())
        thing = self.hasItem(noun)
        if thing != None:
            room.putIn(thing)
            self.items.remove(thing)
            print('You drop a',noun.lower())
        else:
            print('You do not have a',noun.lower(),'to drop!')

    def useItem(self,item):
        if not self.hasItem(item):
            print('You do not have a',item.lower())
        elif item == "KNIFE" and
self.game.getRoom(self.getRoom()).ifContains('SACKS'):
```

```python
                thing = self.game.getRoom(self.getRoom()).ifContains('SACKS')
                print("The sacks disintegrate into scraps. There was nothing in them after all!")
                thing.setShortDesc("scraps")
                thing.setLongDesc("scraps of cloth that may once have been sacks.")
            elif item == "HAMMER" and self.getRoom() == 9:
                print('hurrah!')
                room = self.game.getRoom(self.getRoom())
                if room.getExits() == {}:
                    print('You bash away at the wall with your hammer')
                    time.sleep(2)
                    print('The wall comes down!')
                    room.addExit('NORTH',8)
                    room.setLongDesc("The port midships is the port side of the middle of the ship. The foremast and mainast stretch way, way, way above you. A rough hole has been based in the North wall.")
                    room = self.game.getRoom(8)
                    room.addExit('SOUTH',9)
                    room.setLongDesc("The starboard midships is the starboard side of the middle of the ship, smack between the main mast and the foremast. Just ripe for anything falling from the masts to land on your noggin. A rough hole has been bashed in the South wall.")
            #Else is using something you have, but it does nothing.
            else:
                print('You think about using a',item.lower(),'but this does not seem like the right kind of place to do so.')


    def move(self,direction):
        room = self.game.getRoom(self.getRoom())
        exits = room.getExits()
        if direction in exits.keys():
            print('\nYou move.\n')
            self.room = exits[direction]
            self.look()
        else:
            print('I cannot move that way')
        if self.room == 23:
            time.sleep(2)
            print('In fact... it is *really* slippy here!')
            time.sleep(2)
            print('A bit ... tooo.... slipppppyyy......')
            time.sleep(2)
            print('SPLASH!')
            time.sleep(2)
            print('What is that triangle in the water?')
            time.sleep(2)
            print('CHOMP!!')
```

```python
                self.kill()
        elif self.room == 1:
            if self.hasItem("COIN"):
                print('You ponder')
                time.sleep(2)
                print('You reach into your pocket and pull out the golden coin.')
                time.sleep(2)
                print('You flick the coin in the air and... WHIZZZZZZ!')
                time.sleep(2)
                print('You find yourself teleported to the nicest of pirate islands, surrounded by gold and rum and ... gold...')
                time.sleep(2)
                print('YOU WIN! Well done :)')
                self.game.flipPlayStatus()
            else:
                print("This feels like a really opportune kind of place. You're just sure that with a little money in your pocket you could really make something of yourself from here.")

    def listItems(self):
        count = 0
        print('Things you are holding:')
        for item in self.items:
            print('-',item.getShortDesc())
            count += 1
        if count == 0:
            print('- Nothing!')

    def doCommand(self,verb,noun):
        if verb == 'HELP':
            self.help()
        elif verb == 'LOOK':
            if noun == None:
                self.look()
            else:
                self.lookItem(noun)
        elif verb == 'MOVE':
            self.move(noun)
        elif verb == 'GET':
            self.getItem(noun)
        elif verb == 'DROP':
            self.dropItem(noun)
        elif verb == 'USE':
            self.useItem(noun)
        elif verb == 'CHEAT':
            self.room = int(noun)
        elif verb == 'ITEMS':
            self.listItems()
        else:
```

```python
            print('Unknown verb or noun...')

    def help(self):
        print('Commands:')
        print('LOOK: Look around the current room.')
        print('LOOK <item>: Looks at a specified item.')
        print('MOVE <direction>: Move in the given direction')
        print('GET <item>: Tries to pick up an item.')
        print('DROP <item>: Tries to drop an item.')
        print('USE <item>: Tries to use an item.')
        print('ITEMS: Lists the items you are carrying.')

    def getCommand(self):
        command = input('What do you want to do? ').upper()
        commands = command.split(' ')
        while True:
            if len(commands) == 1:
                verb = commands[0]
                self.doCommand(verb,None)
                break
            elif len(commands) == 2:
                verb = commands[0]
                noun = commands[1]
                self.doCommand(verb,noun)
                break
            else:
                print('Please enter a verb followed by an optional noun.')
                print('Enter HELP for help.')
```

ROOM.py
```python
#An initial definition of a room
class Room:
    #Initiiaslisation happens when you take this description and make it into
    #an object.
    # - self - all class definitions need this so that it can look at it's own properties & methods
    # - id - we will give it a number to identify itt by
    # - shortDesc will be the 'name' of the room
    # - exits will be a list of exits from the room
    # - contains will be a list of the things contained in the room
    # - longDesc will be the longer description which we will only see if we actually look around.
    #   as this is not strictly neccesary, we start it as nothing and then set it later if we
    #   so wish.
    def __init__(self, id, shortDesc, exits, contains):
        self.id = id
        self.shortDesc = shortDesc
```

```python
        self.exits = exits
        self.contains = contains
        self.longDesc = ''

    #This will look at itself and give us back the ID
    def getId(self):
        return self.id #just give back whatever the ID is


    #This will look at itself and give us back the short description
    def getShortDesc(self):
        return self.shortDesc #just give back whatever the current short description is

    #This will take the new description we give it and set this as the object's short description
    def setShortDesc(self,desc):
        self.shortDesc = desc

    #This will look at itself and give us back the long description
    def getLongDesc(self):
        return self.longDesc #Just give back whatever the current long desc is

    #This will take the new description we give it and set this as the object's long description
    def setLongDesc(self,desc):
        self.longDesc = desc

    #This give us a list of exits
    def getExits(self):
        return self.exits

    #This allows us to add a new exit direction which points to the ID of whatever room we wish
    def addExit(self,exitDirection,exitID):
        self.exits.update({exitDirection:exitID})

    #This will give us a list of things the room contains
    def getContains(self):
        return self.contains

    #This will let us test if a particular item is in the room
    def ifContains(self,lookingFor):
        items = self.getContains()
        for item in items:
            if item.getShortDesc().upper() == lookingFor:
                return item
        return None
```

```python
    #This lets us remove an item from the room
    def remove(self,item):
        self.contains.remove(item)

    #This lets us put an item in to the room
    def putIn(self,item):
        self.contains.append(item)
```

THING.py
```python
#An initial definition of a thing
class Thing:
    def __init__(self, id, shortDesc, longDesc, gettable = True):
        self.id = id
        self.shortDesc = shortDesc
        self.longDesc = longDesc
        self.gettable = gettable

    #This will look at itself and give us back the ID
    def getId(self):
        return self.id #just give back whatever the ID is

    #This will look at itself and give us back the short description
    def getShortDesc(self):
        return self.shortDesc #just give back whatever the current short description is

    #This will take the new description we give it and set this as the object's short description
    def setShortDesc(self,desc):
        self.shortDesc = desc

    #This will look at itself and give us back the long description
    def getLongDesc(self):
        return self.longDesc #Just give back whatever the current long desc is

    #This will take the new description we give it and set this as the object's long description
    def setLongDesc(self,desc):
        self.longDesc = desc

    #This will toggle the gettability of the thing
    def toggleGettable(self):
        self.gettable = not self.gettable

    #This will return weather a thing can be got
    def isGettable(self):
        return self.gettable
```

Printed in Great Britain
by Amazon